35⁰⁰

By Southern Hands

By Southern Hands

A Celebration of Craft Traditions in the South

Jan Arnow

A Roundtable Press Book

Oxmoor House, Birmingham

A Roundtable Press Book
Directors: Marsha Melnick, Susan E. Meyer
Project Editor: Virginia Croft
Assistant Editor: Marguerite Ross
Designer: Ronald Gross
Front and Back Cover Photos: Jan Arnow

Oxmoor House, Inc.
P.O. Box 2463
Birmingham, AL 35201
Executive Editor: Candace N. Conard
Production Manager: Jerry Higdon

Photo credits appear on page 236

Frontis photo: Honeysuckle
and split-oak basket made by
North Carolina Cherokee
basketmaker, Linda George

Library of Congress Catalog Number:
87-060993
ISBN: 0-8487-0711-7
Manufactured in the United States of America
First Edition

In memory of my father, with gratitude and love

CONTENTS

INTRODUCTION

All indigenous crafts have inherent traditions in common: people tend to work with materials they have at hand; they tend to fabricate what they see around them; and they tend to produce things they need. The American South has a particularly rich heritage of craft traditions resulting from the confluence of diverse cultures—Native American, European, and African—which adapted to a new environment and often borrowed from one another. All looked to themselves in large measure to provide for their own necessities and pleasures. By the end of the nineteenth century, however, inexpensive factory-made products released people from the often laborious and tedious processes necessary to produce items such as crockery, quilts, and even toys. As the need for self-sufficiency diminished, so did many craft traditions.

Today a few forms of traditional Southern crafts have survived and thrived. Many others, however, are succumbing to attrition as rapidly as are the native materials used in making them. Although many traditional craftspeople are still working throughout the South, the skills so carefully passed from generation to generation are no longer being taught or learned. The younger people have had neither the opportunity nor the need to incorporate handcrafted objects into their lives and so have no idea how, or even why, they were made. And, ironically, many of the craftspeople themselves have contributed to the demise of their traditions by helping their youngsters to "escape" a hard life to a better one through education outside their communities. Today, for the most part, only the elderly remember what was made and how it was done. Their sad refrain that no one is taking up the work is typified by Susan Denson, a Louisiana Choctaw basketmaker: "The young people have been taught basketweaving, but are not interested to see it continue. So after our life, that will be the end of the Choctaw basket."

I began my work on *By Southern Hands* with a lifetime interest in the handmade object. My brother and I were encouraged by our parents at an early age to value the pride of creation over the pride of ownership. The research for this book, then, was a personal odyssey for me, an opportunity to explore the South, my adopted home, for evidence of the strong craft traditions I knew to be there and to meet face to face with the craftspeople themselves.

In pursuit of this vast subject, I immersed myself in a long-standing yet rapidly evolving body of academic material. I discovered, for example, that the term *folklore* was coined as far back as 1846 by British antiquarian William Thoms. At one time the term referred specifically to spoken or performed folk traditions such as stories, songs, or legends. Often used interchangeably with the term *folklife*, today folklore is an area of study that includes all the living traditions of ethnic, regional, occupational, and family groups, expanded to include literature, art, and crafts.

The definition of what is traditional and what is not is as elusive as the definition of art.

Through my work on *By Southern Hands*, I have observed four characteristics that recur among traditional crafts:

1. The quality that distinguishes traditional crafts most clearly from other crafts is that traditional forms of expression are learned and maintained by word of mouth or by observation and imitation, not by formal training.

2. Traditional crafts eschew innovation, tending to follow patterns and forms that are repeated and perpetuated from generation to generation.

3. There is a traditional process by which the methods and patterns are produced, often one that involves hand tools.

4. The objects are made using traditional materials, usually those that are indigenous to a particular area.

Rarely did I find all four characteristics present in any one craft. The economic and ecologic changes of the last one hundred years have left virtually nothing completely untouched. The effects of these changes may signal merely another ebb in the production of traditional crafts, or they may be the flood tide of their demise.

The distinction between art and craft is an issue I dealt with throughout the creation of this book. The term *folk art* refers primarily to the tangible aesthetic or artistic expressions of a group, and *folk craft* usually refers to things that are more utilitarian in nature. The distinction tends to be purely personal. Although collectors invariably (and, it seems, almost seasonally) consider a changing variety of objects such as decoys, rocking chairs, and rag dolls to be desirable for their artistic merit, the craftspeople think of the objects as primarily useful.

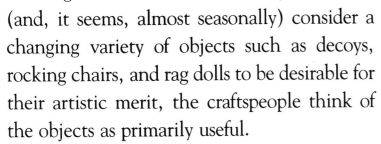

Throughout these last several years, I have conducted research through a variety of sources, including arts councils, state folklore departments, craft guilds, state chambers of commerce, educational institutions, archives, museums, galleries, folklore centers, and folklife festivals. With the help of my research assistant, Jim Young, I have collected and read over 800 bibliographic references. Without benefit of any type of grant or outside funding, I logged more than 50,000 miles, shot more than 6,000 slides, and taped dozens of oral histories.

Nothing in my activity was as important, nor personally so rewarding, as my visits to the homes, shops, and studios of the craftspeople themselves—people who were conspicuously grateful for the opportunity to reveal something of themselves and their work in an atmosphere of respect and interest. With a grace and directness rare in today's world, they entrusted to me their innermost thoughts and feelings about their work and traditions.

The professional folklorists I've been privileged to meet have aggressively sought to protect these craftspeople from outside influences, often including my own. I have personally witnessed the tragic devastation caused by well-intentioned but careless patronage, and I share the folklorists' passionate concern for the lives and work of traditional craftspeople as a vulnerable trust. At the same time, however, I admit to finding myself incapable of forming a relationship other than in the present. Despite their links to the past, each craftsperson I met lived very much in the present. To treat anyone as an artifact would have been unkind and, for me, impossible.

By Southern Hands is not meant to be a definitive work listing every traditional craftsperson in every Southern state, but rather a suggestive overview of the enormous scope of what still exists, however changed or endangered. While containing extensive resources, it is not meant to be a directory of the specific places to find the people shown herein and often, in fact, consciously conceals their exact localities. Nor is it meant to be simply a romantic view of the survival of these folk traditions as seen through the filmy lens of a sentimentalist. These are stories about living Southern craftspeople, about human beings whose lives and work are distinctly intertwined.

In photographing and writing *By Southern Hands*, my goal has been to speak to the present and the future while respecting the past. It has been to suggest that *contemporary* and *traditional* are not mutually exclusive and that neither holds the key to vitality or longevity. My hope is that, through this book, the craft traditions of the South and the local cultures from which they spring will be better understood and preserved.

BASKETMAKING

South Carolina native Mary Alice Scott continues the Gullah basket-sewing tradition passed down to her by her mother and grandmother.

Basketry is one of the oldest known crafts in the world. Some archeologists believe that the making of baskets occurred even before the making and use of pottery. Basket specimens uncovered in American digs have been dated at about 5000 B.C. Since such ancient times until only a few generations ago, people have intertwined whatever materials were immediately available into useful, durable containers essential to every household.

The very early European settlers in America combined the basketry skills they brought from their native countries with techniques they learned from the Native Americans. In contrast, the basketry traditions brought by slaves from Africa remained distinct. Yet each tradition—European, Indian, and African—was centered on meeting the everyday needs of rural farm life. Baskets were used to carry seed to the fields for planting, to hold crops during harvesting, and to take them to market. Grain was measured, feathers collected, and animals carried in baskets.

Some baskets were tightly woven from splits of sturdy oak and used as heavy-duty carriers. Some were woven in a double layer of river cane or in a single layer and coated with pine tar to hold and carry water. Others were woven loosely in shallow forms to use as sieves, or shaped into a cone with a tapered point to place in rapid streams to catch fish.

Basketmaking tended to be a family enterprise involving even the youngest children. Whether the culture was European, African, or Native American in origin, the techniques were handed down from generation to generation. As opportunities for trade developed, many basketmakers lived on a barter economy and survived lean times by swapping their extra baskets for food or other items they did not produce themselves.

"Back in those days there was no money," recalls Edmund Youngbird, a member of the Eastern Band of the Cherokee Indians. "Mother and Grandmother used to go out walking toward Shoal Creek with a load of baskets tied in a sheet. Mama would trade for chickens, beans, pumpkins, and eggs. A neighbor would let Mama use his wagon to carry merchandise she had received in exchange for her baskets."

The economic changes of the twentieth century radically altered the Southern basketmaking traditions. In the early part of the century the new lumber industry destroyed many of the plants and trees that had provided the raw materials for basketmaking. The Depression forced farmers to seek jobs off the land, further eroding handcraft traditions. And finally, factory-made items—galvanized buckets, paper bags, and inexpensive plastic containers—all but eradicated the need for handmade baskets.

Throughout the Southern Native American communities in the early 1940s, interest in basketmaking was rekindled by economic programs introduced by the Bureau of Indian Affairs. These programs, designed to supplement the income of Native American communities, placed new emphasis on the handcraft traditions. In addition, they brought a new force to the enterprise: marketing. With sales outlets for their baskets, the Indians shifted the focus of their craft from the utilitarian to the more decorative.

Despite these influences and accommodations, basketry continues as a highly developed Southern craft, rooted in rich traditions. It is still possible to find intricate patterns of Cherokee river cane, fragrant coils of South Carolina sweet grass, and delicate splits of Appalachian white oak being produced today.

SPLIT-OAK BASKETS

Unknown Sitter, *ca. 1934, by Doris Ulmann.*

When we think of oak, images of towering, rigid trees come to mind, trees that provide the lumber to build churches, bridges, and furniture. It is not difficult to understand, then, that the thin, pliable strips peeled from oak trees have produced some of the most durable baskets imaginable. Because the strength of split oak is equaled by a surprising pliability, it was employed to make baskets for a variety of functions, ranging from huge, round hampers used for collecting cotton to small "cheek" or "hip" baskets—formed by a deeply indented center rib into two sections—used for collecting eggs.

Although baskets made of oak splits, or wood peelings are common to almost all traditional communities in the South, the bountiful supplies of white oak in the mountains and valleys of Kentucky, Tennessee, and North Carolina have made it easy for residents in those areas to maintain the traditions of split-oak basketmaking. There are entire communities, such as those in Cannon County, Tennessee, where almost every family includes either a basketmaker or chairmaker working with white oak and producing the same objects as their forebears did.

Mary Prater, who lives on Short Mountain near the small town of Woodbury in Cannon County, continues to make baskets the way she learned as a child. Using a few simple tools, she creates both burden and domestic baskets by starting from scratch with the growing tree, "from the pole out," as the local dialect describes it.

Whatever her choice of basket, the selection of the tree is crucial. Although any size and age can be used, the best splits come from straight young saplings, six to eight inches in diameter, with smooth, flat bark. After finding her saplings, she cuts them down, taking back to the woodlot only the six- to nine-foot pole of straight timber that comes from just above the base of the tree to the first limb.

The transformation of these small logs into wood splits that are thin and flexible enough to weave is a slow and tedious process. Using a pair of metal wedges and a mallet, the same tools that have been used for generations to do the same job, she splits each log through its center into eight wedges called "bolts" or "billets." This exposes the heartwood, the core of the tree, which is next removed. Because the heartwood does not split easily, it is put aside for use as ribs, hoops, and handles.

1. *Tennessee basketmaker Mary Prater peels each oak split until no more than 1/16 inch thick.*

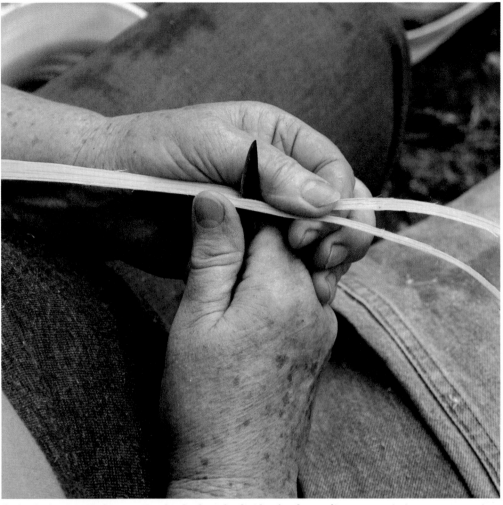

2. *Mrs. Prater then uses her pocketknife to scrape the thin wood free of splinters.*

3. *As the last step before weaving her basket, she divides the clean splits once again into narrow sections only 1/8 inch wide. The oak splits are finally ready to "work into" a basket.*

4. *She weaves the narrow oak splits under and over the ribs, shaping the basket as she weaves.*

After scraping off the bark, she wedges the point of her pocketknife between the tree's annual growth rings at the exposed end of the billet and carefully peels a section apart with her hands. She continues peeling each piece of wood into thinner and thinner splits, pulling the sections apart evenly, until they are no more than 1/16 inch thick.

She then trims the new thin splits to an even width and scrapes each side smooth and free from splinters by drawing the thin wood across her knees under the knife. A padding of old overalls protects her from the sharp blade of the knife. Finally, she separates each sleek split into narrow sections only 1/8 inch wide.

After her materials are prepared, Mary Prater begins her basket by bending two of the strips of heartwood into circles and nailing the two circles together at right angles to each other, one forming the handle and the bottom curve of the basket, and the other one its rim. Using some of the thin splits, she wraps the nailed intersections where the handle and rim are joined. Next, she cuts several ribs from the heartwood, sharpens the ends, and inserts them into the thin split

Virginia Laborers Picking Cotton, *ca. 1890*.

This split-oak basket by Cherokee Indian Dolly Taylor derives its pattern from dyed splits.

Wide oak splits are used by Alabama native Hazel Smith to make a strong picnic basket.

Large baskets originally were used by slaves to collect cotton before the days of mechanized harvesting. Today basketmakers like Hazel Smith make them for use as laundry hampers.

wrappings. Spaced at even intervals, the ribs complete the frame on which she will weave the basket.

All this time, the narrow ⅛-inch splits that she has prepared for "working in" have been soaking in a bucket of water to make them pliable. She uses them now to make the weft of the basket, pulling the splits tight as she weaves, and occasionally she adds more ribs, tucking their ends securely into the woven splits. From preparing the materials to finishing her basket, she typically will spend an entire month.

The preparation of the wood for other types of split

basketry is much the same, but the weaving patterns and surface treatment vary widely. Cotton baskets, once made to carry up to 100 pounds of cotton but now primarily used as laundry and trash baskets, are constructed of much wider splits, which are woven in a simple basketweave pattern, eliminating the need for ribs. Cherokee split-oak basketmakers usually include the extra step of coloring some of their splits with natural dyes to further enhance their patterns.

(Right) Each basket in Mary Prater's extraordinary set of nesting split-oak hip baskets is woven so tightly that light barely penetrates.

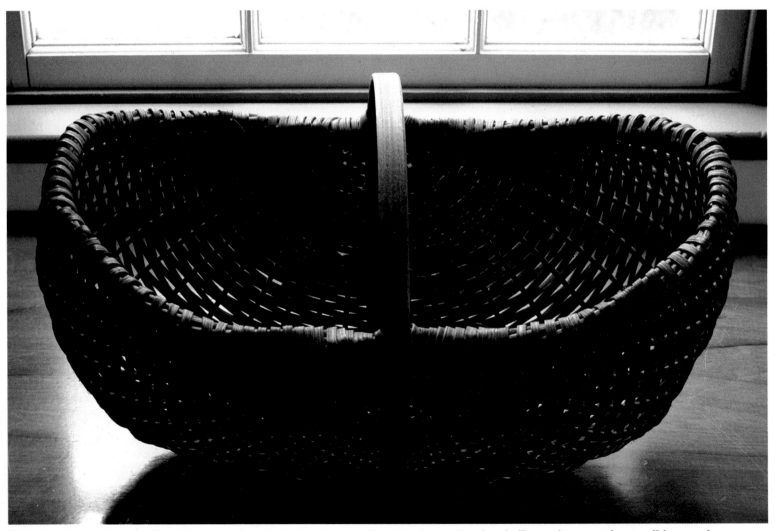

North Carolina basketmaker Pattie Neal dyes the splits in her delicate split-oak baskets with walnut hulls to achieve a rich, overall brown color.

RIVER-CANE BASKETS

Growing densely along the banks and streams of Southern states from Texas to Virginia, common river cane has been the basket material most used by Native Americans in the South. This plant has played a vital role in dozens of Native American cultures, from the Cherokees in the Greak Smoky Mountains to the Chitimachas along the coast in southern Louisiana. They fashioned weapons, tools, building materials, and even hair ornaments from the plant. But of all the skills at which these native peoples excelled, the plaiting of river cane into exquisite baskets remains unequaled. The basketry traditions of the many tribes are among the most highly developed and active in the South today.

Rowena Bradley, a Cherokee recognized as one of the most talented river-cane basket weavers in the United States, learned the craft from her mother at the age of seven. She continues, along with others in her mountain community in western North Carolina, to harvest, prepare, and weave river cane in the Cherokee tradition.

She searches the canebrakes, the dense stands near the swampy areas close to her home, for cane that is at least two years old and has shed its husk-like covering. As the reed shoots up, it grows from joint to joint, growing taller but not increasing in diameter. At about eight feet, it is ready to harvest. "If you cut the cane too young," she explains, "it will be too brittle. If it's too old, it's hard on the hands."

Using only a pocketknife, she harvests as many as fifty "sticks" for a single basket. After carrying the sticks back to her yard, she divides each one into four or more splits. The satiny outer layer is peeled off, and the coarse, inner fiber discarded. She uses the resulting long, narrow splits of cane to weave her baskets.

The natural color of freshly harvested cane is a delicate green, which ages to a deep ochre over time. Unlike Appalachian split-oak baskets, which depend largely upon the natural colors of the materials for their beauty, the surface designs of Native American river-cane baskets are produced by dyeing some of the cane before weaving.

Rowena Bradley's double-walled river-cane basket will hold water, as the cane swells when wet.

Common river cane, shown here in its raw, split, and dyed forms, has been the basket material most often used by Southern Native Americans.

Mrs. Bradley makes her traditional dyes from the trees and roots indigenous to her mountain home—black walnut hulls and roots for brown, bloodroot for orange, butternut root for black, and yellowroot for yellow. She fills a large pot with water and then puts in alternating layers of dye materials and river-cane splits. As the water boils over a wood fire, she turns the cane and dye materials over and over with a wooden stick to dye the splits evenly until the desired color is achieved.

The duration of the dyeing process varies, depending upon the amount of cane being dyed, the strength of the dye, the intensity of color desired, and the choice of dye materials. Although river cane accepts and holds dye easily, it is very dense and requires several hours for the colors to penetrate. Boiling the cane for as many as twelve hours is not unusual.

When the river cane is drained and has cooled, it is ready to be woven. Beginning at the bottom and spanning over and under the framework at varying intervals as she weaves, Mrs. Bradley creates the baskets that have, for generations, been used for storing food, winnowing corn, and harvesting crops. The names of

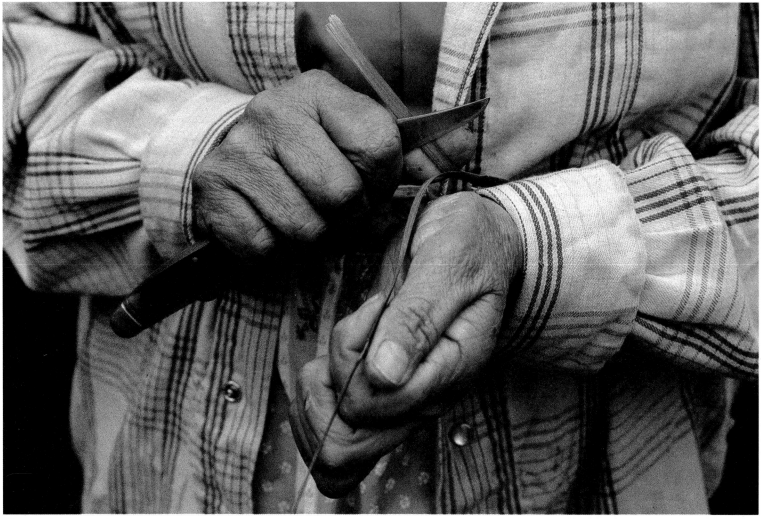

Using only a pocketknife, Cherokee basketmaker Rowena Bradley peels off the satiny outer layer of the cane "stick" for use in making her baskets.

the diagonal patterns are evocative of earlier days—Chief's Daughter, Noon Day Sun, Broken Heart.

Rowena Bradley is especially adept at double-weave basketry, a complex technique in which one basket is woven inside another and the two joined by a seamless edge. When filled with water, the tightly woven double-walled vessel becomes virtually solid as the cane swells. The geometric effect created by the interlocking diagonals of the double walls results in an intricate pattern unrivaled in river-cane basketmaking.

Unlike Mrs. Bradley, who is able to maintain her

dyeing traditions because the ecology of her surroundings is similar to that of her ancestors', the Chitimacha Indians in Louisiana have been forced to adapt their river-cane basketry traditions to changing conditions. This relatively small tribe, living along the Louisiana bayous, has for generations produced some of the most delicately scaled river-cane baskets in the South. Their sources for native dyes, however, have been decimated by chemical sprays used near their river homes, and they have turned to commercially produced dyes to color the cane in their finely crafted baskets.

Rowena Bradley's cane baskets show the distinctive Cherokee patterning made with both natural and dyed cane.

HONEYSUCKLE BASKETS

Honeysuckle, one of the most common plants throughout the South, has only recently been adopted for use by Southern basketmakers. Less than a century ago it was introduced to the South as a material for basketry by immigrants from Japan, where it is commonly used. Although honeysuckle is not strong enough to be used in burden and work baskets, basketmakers from the Ohio River to the Gulf of Mexico have chosen its long, slender stems for making smaller, decorative baskets.

Honeysuckle can be gathered and cut any time of the year, but harvesting is easier during the fall and winter months when leaves do not obscure the vines. The best honeysuckle for basketmaking grows where sunlight is abundant—along roadsides, at the edges of woods, and on fences. Younger vines are preferred because they are often straighter and have fewer branches and also because they are not as hollow and brittle as older vines. No tools are needed to harvest the vines. They are simply broken off near their roots, cleaned of leaves and small branches, and tied in bundles for carrying.

Before the vines can be used for basketmaking, their bark must be removed by scalding. The coiled honeysuckle is covered with water in a deep pan and boiled until the brown outer covering begins to loosen. The bark can then be slipped off easily by rubbing the vines with a rag, and the joints are trimmed smooth with a knife. Some basketmakers bleach the vines to whiten them after boiling, and many use the same natural dyes as used on river cane to color the vines prior to weaving.

Honeysuckle is most easily harvested during the winter months when leaves do not hide the vines.

HONEYSUCKLE BASKETS

Many honeysuckle basketmakers use ribs of split oak to add strength to their baskets.

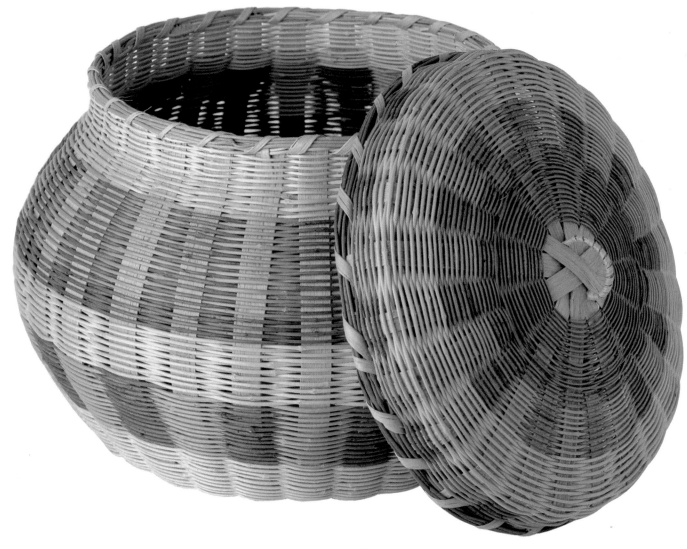

TWIG & VINE BASKETS

In sharp contrast to the tedious preparation of split oak is the relatively easy use of various smaller plants in the construction of twisted-twig baskets. River willow, grapevine, and other easily gathered sprigs require little or no processing and consequently are popular basketmaking materials throughout the South. Although not as strong as split-oak baskets, these more swiftly made stick and vine containers have nevertheless provided Southern families with durable receptacles for generations.

River willow, which grows abundantly in marshy areas near creeks and streams, is similar in appearance to the drooping streamers of the more familiar weeping willow but is a much stronger variety. Baskets produced from weeping willow limbs crumble shortly after drying, but those made from river willow retain their shape and durability for many years.

River willow is most easily cut after the first frost when the sap is no longer running and when snakes that live in the same areas have begun their hibernation. The best sprouts, called "weavers," are no more than ⅛ inch thick and can be as long as three feet. After harvesting, the weavers must be kept damp or they will peel and crack when they are worked into a basket. Some basketmakers keep stacks of the sprouts in their freezers to retain their moisture for use throughout the year. Others work with river willow only during the fall and winter seasons, harvesting weavers every few weeks, and switch to different materials for making their baskets during the spring and summer months.

The most common form of river-willow basket is made by first soaking two slender branches of hickory or dogwood until they are pliable and then bending them into circles that are joined at right angles like the frame of a split-oak basket. Strips of hickory bark are wrapped around the intersections of the two circles, and then ribs whittled from more dogwood limbs are inserted into the bark-wrapped corners to complete the frame. The willow is woven over and under the ribs, covering them as completely as possible, until the basket is completed.

Grapevines are also harvested most often when the sap is down, and are abundant on trees and fences along rural roadways. Basketmakers look for the newest growth closest to the ground for the most pliable weavers. If gathered in the summer, they must be bleached to kill the insects inhabiting them. The consequences of omitting this step can be disastrous. As Norma Walters, an eastern Kentucky basketmaker, warns, "Otherwise they bore little holes in the vine and you have a pile of sawdust right where the basket was sitting."

Grapevine baskets are most often created by one of two easy methods. In the first, a simple framework of intersecting twigs is constructed and the grapevines are woven in and out of the frame, producing lightweight containers used primarily as decorative accessories.

In the second method, several vines are twisted together to make a thick ring, which is wrapped tightly with more vines. Additional rings are constructed in the same manner. The rings are stacked on top of one another to form the sides of the basket, and a vine or thin branch is woven in and out to hold them together. For the handle, several thicker vines are looped through opposite edges of the basket, and the bottom is formed by forcing twigs through and across the lowest ring.

Kentucky basketmaker Danny Yocum easily and quickly constructs twig and vine baskets from river willow, grapevines, and other supple plant materials.

River-willow baskets are both durable and strong.

Twig baskets are made by coiling bundles of shoots into rings and then stacking them on top of one another.

Another method is to construct a frame of short, intersecting twigs and then weave vines in and out of the framework, creating light, airy baskets.

BARK BASKETS

Not all baskets are formed of woven, twined, or coiled materials. Some of the most remarkable containers are constructed simply of whole pieces of poplar, hickory, or birch bark held together with bark lacings, and others completely of the lacings themselves. Characteristic of all baskets of this type is their relatively fast and simple construction.

The diameter of the tree determines the size of the whole pieces of bark that can be used. With a pocketknife, the basketmaker makes two horizontal slits across the outer bark, cutting just enough for the dimensions of the finished basket. Using the tip of the knife, he or she lifts the cut edge, separating it from the tree, then simply peels the sheet of outer bark from the tree, an easy task if the sap is running and the bark is pliable.

These broad sheets of bark can be bent into shapes as simple as the stapled containers found at roadside fruit stands or as sublime as the ingeniously molded mountain berry basket shown on page 33, which is designed to sit comfortably on the knee as the collected berries are culled.

The lacing used on bark baskets can be pulled either from the outer layer of bark or from the inner layer, referred to as the "bast." As one elderly North Carolina basketmaker explains, "You can take your knife, nick off a piece right down at the bottom of a young hickory sapling, and start walking backwards, pulling it. It strips right up to the top of the tree!"

These hickory lacings are also occasionally used to weave a crudely constructed rib-and-split basket, which is roughly similar to the more refined split-oak variety. A frame is built of wooden splits wrapped together at the joints with thin lacings of hickory bark. To fill out the frame, twig ribs are whittled to a point on their ends and pushed into the wrapping.

The remaining bark is boiled, and the dark, softened outer bark removed, leaving the inner strips as pliable as glove leather. These broad strips of hickory bark are then woven through the wood and twig framework to complete the basket.

A sheet of poplar bark, with lichens and moss left on the surface, was used to form a handsome North Carolina basket, laced with hickory bark.

The leather-like strips that Cherokee basketmaker Lucinda Reed uses to weave unusual half-baskets are actually long pieces of inner bark from a hickory tree.

A simple over-and-under weave can be used to construct a bark quiver or other tall baskets.

HUCKLEBUCKETS

Not all baskets are made to last a lifetime. One form of bark basket, the traditional mountain berry basket, or hucklebucket, has a lifetime that rarely lasts a week!

Bea Thomas, whose husband, Luther, made one of the baskets pictured on this page, recalls: "People traveled across the mountains here in North Carolina on foot in the old days. These mountains were just spiderwebbed with hard-beaten paths from people going back and forth. Often they'd come across a patch of wild berries they wanted to carry home. They'd just peel off a piece of poplar bark the approximate size they wanted their basket, score the outside of it, bend it up, and lace it with hickory bark. After they got home, they didn't have any more use for it, so they'd use it for kindling!"

PINE-NEEDLE BASKETS

The longleaf pine tree, sometimes called the Southern pine, is found from southern Virginia to Florida and west into Texas. Its long, graceful needles grow in clusters of three, forming dense tufts. The needles, or "pine straw" as they are regionally known, which average from eight to eighteen inches in length, have been used by basketmakers in the deep South for many generations.

One of the strongest continuing pine-needle basket traditions is maintained by Louisiana's Coushatta Indians. The name Coushatta actually means "white reed brake," which refers to the lush basket cane of their original northern Alabama homeland. During colonial expansion, they were forced to migrate to Louisiana, where cane was scarce. Substituting a coiling technique for weaving, they adapted their basketry traditions to their new home and its indigenous materials. For several generations after relocating, the Coushattas made coiled baskets of long grasses sewn together with the inner bark of the dogwood tree. By the late 1930s, however, changing agricultural conditions forced them to switch to the more available pine needles sewn with raffia, a palm material imported from Madagascar.

The long pine needles are gathered locally, either harvested directly off the tree when the needles have attained their full summer growth or gathered from the ground in the early fall. They must be thoroughly dried for several months before use, as a basket made with fresh needles will shrink and loosen when it dries.

After the needles are separated from their clusters and cleaned of chaff and dirt, the baskets are begun by bundling together several needles and coiling them in a tight spiral. Each row is then laid along the edge of the preceding row. Raffia is wrapped around the bundle of needles in the row and stitched to the last row, forming a distinctive radiating pattern. The Coushattas' craftsmanship in making fine baskets with snug-fitting lids reaches its zenith in animal baskets that resemble crabs, alligators, ducks, and other animals or birds.

The long needles of the Southern pine average more than a foot in length.

Each pine-needle basket is begun as a tight coil of long needles wrapped with strips of dried palmetto or raffia.

The needles, known locally as "pine straw," are harvested right from the tree during late summer or from the ground in early fall. They are thoroughly dried, then soaked to make them pliable before use.

Floridian Irene Foreman decorates the lids of her baskets by making tiny knots of pine needles.

A life-size turkey made from pine needles, raffia, and pine-cone petals by Coushatta Indian Lorena Langley serves as a spectacular example of the Louisiana tribe's many effigy baskets.

SWEET-GRASS BASKETS

Mrs. Green Winnowing Her Rice, *ca. 1909, by Leigh Rich-mond Miner.*

The drive south along the stretch of Highway 17 from Mount Pleasant to Charleston, South Carolina, provides welcome relief from the proliferation of shopping malls, fast-food restaurants, and garish signage usually found along such roads. Instead, the roadside is dotted with dozens of simple wooden stands, each festooned with intricately coiled sweet-grass baskets. The creators of these baskets, descendants of the slaves who worked South Carolina's rice plantations, are the only group of black craftspeople to continue a tradition that is now several hundred years old.

On plantations along the coastal region of South Carolina called the lowcountry, vital roles were performed by the slaves who brought basketry skills from their west African homelands. Coiled baskets made by the slaves from bulrushes and sweet grass were used everywhere on the plantation, from the rice fields to the Big House. One basket form, the fanner basket used for winnowing the rice, was brought directly from

Africa. Others, such as the wall-mounted half-baskets, were influenced by European forms that the slaves copied. Derivatives of all these shapes can still be found today along Highway 17.

By the early 1900s, with slave labor abolished by the Civil War and the land torn apart by a series of devastating hurricanes and floods between 1893 and 1916, the rice plantations were in ruins. Many of the freed slaves, however, began farming and continued to produce baskets for their own use.

Around 1930, in order to supplement their income, "basket sewers," as those who produced coiled baskets were known, began making show baskets for sale to tourists, displaying them along the increasingly traveled highway to Charleston. Today they are also found in the town itself at Four Corners of the Law (where four government buildings sit on opposing corners) and in the Old Slave Market on Market Street.

All of the materials used in Mount Pleasant coiled baskets—the sweet grass and bulrush that are the

Sweet grass, the slender wild grass used as the foundation for most Gullah baskets, once grew abundantly in the marshlands of South Carolina. Today the lush stands are endangered by commercial and residential building.

Most sweet-grass baskets are started with a tight coil of flexible pine needles. The coil is continued by adding strands of sweet grass and bulrush, which are bound with lengths of dried palmetto.

foundation materials; the longleaf pine needles that begin the coils and provide color variation; and the palmetto fronds that bind the coils together—are indigenous to the lowcountry and are used in their natural state without bleaching or dyeing.

The baskets are usually begun in the center with a tight coiling of pine needles that changes to the less flexible grass or rush as the diameter expands. They are built coil upon coil, the grass or rush circling upon itself. Using a tool called a "bone"—a sharpened instrument usually made from a spoon whose bowl has been removed—the basket sewer pierces the preceding coil and inserts a strip of palmetto frond, or "binder," which is pulled tightly around the individual coil, binding it to the growing basket. More grass or rush is added as needed, and each row bound and connected to the preceding one. The binding fronds form radiating rows of stitching in a manner similar to Coushatta pine-needle baskets. Sometimes the basket sewers add a decorative touch by tying small knots in thin bundles of pine needles and laying them in the foundation as it is sewn into the basket.

Mary Alice Scott, a fifth-generation basket sewer in South Carolina, sews baskets daily beside her stand on Highway 17.

*Beehive or mountain basket by
Louisa Nelson.*

*Hinged sewing basket by
Mary Alice Scott.*

(Above) *Elizabeth Mazyck created this unusual rectangular basket on an oval foundation by bending, but not breaking, the corners of the bulrush as she coiled it.* (Left) *The contrast between the stark white strips of palmetto and the subtle greens and browns of the sweet grass, bulrush, and pine needles creates exciting displays of baskets in the Old Slave Market in Charleston, South Carolina.*

Palmetto Baskets

The palmetto palm grows wild throughout the deep South but is especially abundant in marshy areas near rivers and streams. In nearly every community where palmetto has grown, its fronds have been harvested for use as a building material and as binding strands for native grass basketry. In all the South, however, only in Louisiana has the palmetto been used as the primary material for baskets and other items.

It is not known whether the Native Americans in Louisiana taught the French and Acadian settlers to work with the material or whether the immigrants taught the Indians. Whichever is the case, palmetto braiding today remains as the most prominent craft form of the Houma Indians, the largest surviving group of Native Americans living in Louisiana.

Florestine Billiot plaits and then sews palmetto strands to create her open baskets, which are traditional among the Houma Indians in Louisiana.

Only the heart of the palmetto plant, le coeur, *is cut for palmetto weaving, just before it opens into its characteristic fan.*

The fronds are sometimes left to dry for several days on a window screen.

In the southeastern Louisiana community of Dulac, along the high, narrow banks of the Bayou Grand Caillou, a small group of elderly Houma women continue the palmetto traditions they learned as young girls from their mothers and grandmothers. One of them, Marie Dean, braids yards and yards of palmetto every day, then coils and sews the braided strands into baskets, hats, and fans.

She harvests her palmetto from grounds near her home on the bayou, cutting only the heart, *le coeur*, before the fronds have opened to their characteristic fan. Once they open, she explains, the fronds are too stiff to braid. After cutting, she allows them to dry in the sun for several weeks.

When she is ready to begin a basket, she carefully slits the individual fronds into ¼-inch strands and begins to braid. The number of strips she uses in the braid ranges from three to as many as seven, depending on the style and design of her finished piece.

Once she feels that she has braided a sufficient amount of palmetto, she carefully coils the braid, overlapping the edges and sewing the rows together with brightly colored thread. Each basket or hat may take as many as sixty feet of braid!

Miss Dean also makes dolls, using Spanish moss, another abundant indigenous plant. She collects the moss from trees around her home and washes it in the bayou to get it clean. She mounds it in her backyard and lets it cure for several weeks, turning the mound over every few days to allow it to dry evenly. When its gray outer coating drops off and the black cortex is completely visible, the moss has dried sufficiently and is ready for her to fashion into the dolls, which she then dresses in braided palmetto clothing or places in palmetto cradles.

Houma Indian Marie Dean plaits five strands of split palmetto into a length as long as sixty feet before coiling it into a hat or a basket.

(Right) Florestine Billiot coils and sews her long plaited palmetto strand into an open-topped basket.

Patterns in Basketweaving

Basketmaking began before recorded history to fill a need for durable, lightweight, easily constructed containers. Practical reminders of more difficult times, baskets continue to be made today, but are appreciated more for their aesthetic than their utilitarian qualities. Basketmakers in the South have developed construction techniques that most appropriately complement their raw materials—trees, vines, roots, bark, grasses, leaves—and the result is a great variety of patterns and forms.

Twilling, or diagonal weaving, the most commonly used method in Cherokee, Chitimacha, and Choctaw cane basketry, allows for complex patterning by simple in-and-out weaving of the relatively inflexible cane. Bold, allover patterns are possible because the cane can be easily dyed.

Unlike twilling, coiling depends on the natural colors and textures of native sweet grass, bulrush, and palmetto to produce the spiral designs typical of low-country South Carolina baskets. More supple than cane, grasses and pine needles are easy to manipulate, presenting greater possibilities for ornamentation.

Traditional split-oak baskets, usually left undyed, are sturdy, durable containers made from materials of enormous strength. Their patterns depend on the width of the splits, some as narrow as ¹⁄₁₆ inch, and the tightness of the simple weave around oak ribs. Larger split-oak baskets, such as the old cotton hampers, begin at the bottom as radiating spokes of wide splits that are plainly woven as the basket is curved upward.

Light, airy containers, less useful as burden baskets yet no less beautiful, can be made with slender, less hardy materials such as honeysuckle. Often they are woven on a rigid frame, with the flexible material used as the weft.

The criteria by which the quality of a basket can be judged vary according to the materials and techniques used in its construction. In split-oak work, for example, the tightness of the weave and the width and even quality of the splits might be considered, as well as the smoothness of the handle. In a sweet-grass basket, even stitching, strong tension, and an interesting pattern are desirable qualities. All baskets, are judged on the symmetry and balance of their forms.

Dyed and natural woven river cane forms a twilled herringbone pattern.

Plainly woven split oak, both natural and dyed.

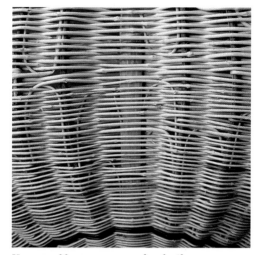

Honeysuckle woven around oak ribs.

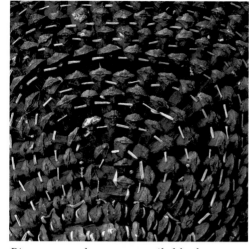

Pine-cone petals sewn to a coiled basket.

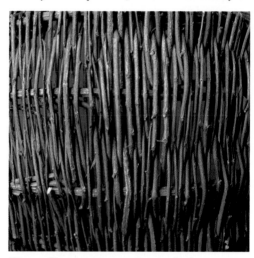

River willow woven over dogwood ribs.

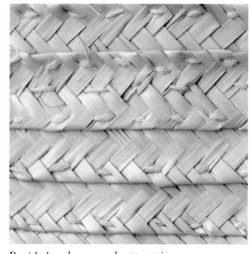

Braided and sewn palmetto strip.

River cane twilled into a complex pattern.

Bottom of a split-oak cotton basket.

Split oak woven over split-oak ribs.

Coiled basket sewn with palmetto strips.

CORN-SHUCK BAGS

Willie London learned to make things from corn shucks when he was in elementary school in southeastern Louisiana, but he did not begin working with them in earnest until he was a young father needing a bag to hold his first child's diapers while the family attended church. He constructed one by twisting and knotting together corn shucks and eventually made a bag for each of his ten children and all of his grandchildren. Since then his craft has evolved from simple diaper bags to imaginative and stylish purses and portfolios.

All of his creations are made exclusively from corn shucks that are twisted tightly into twine. To begin a bag, he attaches one end of the corn-shuck twine to a flat, wooden block. After winding the twine twice around the block form, he ties a series of connecting half-hitch knots, adding more twisted shucks as needed. He knots row after row, turning the block over and over as he builds up the bag. When he has completed the piece, he cuts off the twine and tucks the end into the preceding knots to prevent unraveling.

Some of his bags are open-ended, and others have long tops that are folded over and fastened with a changing variety of fasteners, which have included pieces of tin cut from beer cans and Mardi Gras "coins" called doubloons. The handles on his bags are made separately and then attached.

No longer needing to produce carrying bags for his own family, he now attends fairs and festivals throughout Louisiana, demonstrating his technique and selling the bags.

Working with two strands of corn shucks, Willie London twists them into a twine, which he then tightly knots, row after row, around a wooden form.

Mr. London's bags are no longer used as plain, utilitarian carriers but instead are now stylishly designed, many with folded tops and shoulder straps.

Working at the New Orleans Jazz and Heritage Festival, Mr. London sells his bags to fairgoers who are attracted to his one-of-a-kind handwork.

TOYMAKING

Although the pervasive Puritan attitudes of the early settlers discouraged frivolous amusement, religiously acceptable toys like Noah's Ark were allowed.

Anyone who has watched a small child lift a simple wooden aircraft while making airplane noises or carefully prop a faceless rag doll in a miniature chair and feed it imaginary tea and cakes knows how a toy can effectively stimulate a child's imagination. Toys and games offer endless hours of excitement, fantasy, and adventure while preparing children for the world outside their playrooms. Toys and games provide the turnstile through which every young child passes when entering the real world in later years.

If *work* is defined as those activities that are related to our basic survival needs, then *play* may be viewed as nonproductive. As Mark Twain so aptly expressed in *The Adventures of Tom Sawyer*, "Work consists of whatever a body is 'obliged' to do, and Play consists of whatever a body is not obliged to do." Even though play may not always produce immediately tangible results, it nevertheless has contributed, throughout history, to the psychological, social, and physical development of children and adults of all cultures.

Few historical examples of American toys remain, primarily because toys were made from whatever materials were at hand and were not considered objects important enough to save. Both practical and religious factors, moreover, discouraged the introduction of toys into the life of the American child. It is known that lack of shipboard space prevented the earliest settlers from bringing many toys to America. As they labored to create new homes in the wilderness, they had little time for play, and those children who did not die in infancy worked alongside their parents in the effort to survive. In New England especially, the pervasive Puritan attitudes of the early settlers discouraged frivolous amusement.

Gradually, as life became easier for parents, their attitudes about children changed. A few pieces survive this period. At first, religiously oriented toys were allowed, objects that were directly related to biblical tales. Noah's Ark, for example, was a toy boat with a removable top, inside of which were stored dozens of miniature animals. Children were allowed an increasing variety of playthings, all of which were made by hand from available materials.

The growth of manufacturing after the Civil War also signaled the growth of the commercial toy industry. Wooden sleds, rocking horses, and other items appeared in mail-order catalogs, and general stores stocked more and more factory-made toys. But many people, especially in the isolated mountain communities of the South, could not afford the manufactured toys. They continued to make their own—sewing dolls from scraps of material, whittling animals from scraps of wood, and crafting miniatures of the adult environment from whatever was at hand. These toys were exquisite in their simplicity of design and inventive use of materials.

Today, despite a seemingly endless parade of mass-produced plastic toys shrink-wrapped for sale in cavernous toy stores, there are people who still believe that a child can be endlessly entertained by less complicated, handmade toys. Today's handmade toys are similar to the historical examples. They bear a striking resemblance to their antecedents, delightfully evocative of childhood. These toymakers continue to rely on native materials and the memories of their own childhood toys to produce wonderful alternatives to the flashy plastic objects touted by the media. As one mountain toymaker said, "I've had letters from anthropologists who say these toys are more sophisticated than modern toys. People keep comin' back to them. I think they'll outlast 'em all."

DOLLS

On almost every toy shelf, amid the jumble of games, crayons, and mechanical toys, the face of a doll will peek through. As the favored toy of children since the beginning of recorded history, the doll has served as best friend, confidant, and child of children everywhere. Through fantasy and imaginary role play, dolls have provided both the model and the means by which little children have practiced for entry into the adult world.

Tombs of ancient Egypt have yielded carved and painted dolls with flat, wooden bodies and hair formed of threaded clay beads. As early as six hundred years B.C., the children of ancient Greece played with jointed dolls with movable arms and legs, as did Roman children three centuries later. Dolls from every culture and every era have provided miniature portraits of the dress and customs of the times.

In the year 1585, artist John White sketched a young Native American girl clutching a newly acquired and stylishly fashioned English doll. It had been traded to the Indians by members of his English expedition, which had landed off the coast of North Carolina that year.

This properly dressed English doll, however, was not typical of what most children owned in the early days of this country. More characteristic were the doll forms learned from the Indians and made of materials that were abundant—apples and nuts, corncobs and corn shucks—and decorated with pokeberry juice for the mouths and dots of soot for the eyebrows and hair.

Apple-head dolls, made from carved fresh apples left to dry and shrivel, are one of the traditional doll forms that are still made today. Kentucky dollmaker Marla Steitz, who learned the craft from her great-grandmother, usually makes the heads for her dolls in the autumn, right after the harvest, "because that's when I can find a really good selection of apples."

Because the apples will shrink to half their original size, she begins by choosing a large, firm apple, usually a Red Delicious or Granny Smith. Ignoring small, superficial blemishes, she rejects any apples that have large bruises, which will cause the apple to rot rather than dry out evenly.

She first peels the apple completely, removing any small brown spots with a knife. Before carving the face, she examines the apple for the smoothest and roundest side. Then, with the tip of her knife, she notches out the eyes, digging out sockets in which a black-eyed pea will later fit.

The nose is formed by cutting out a triangle, wide part at the bottom; the mouth is cut in a similar way beneath the nose, and the cheeks are formed by carving out ridges under the eyes. Finally, she trims off some of the sides, giving the apple a tapered effect.

To support the apple while it is drying, she slowly and carefully impales it onto the whittled point of a tree branch, which will serve as the armature for the padded body. "With luck, the apple won't crack," she warns. "If you cut too much away while you're forming the face, you never know what will happen. There's nothing you can do if it does split. Just eat your mistake and start from scratch again!" To retard the natural darkening of the apple, she rolls the head in lemon juice. Then she stands the supported apple head in a jar, allowing air to circulate freely all around it.

Drying time depends on the size and type of apple and the humidity. Some apple-head dollmakers say that drying the heads outdoors makes them age faster,

1. *Kentucky dollmaker Marla Steitz notches out eye sockets with her knife after peeling the apple.*

2. *After completing the facial features, she forms the cheeks by carving out ridges beneath the eyes.*

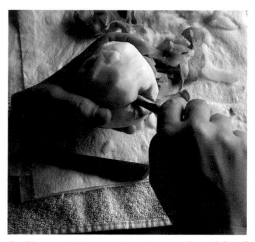

3. *She carefully impales the carved applehead onto the whittled end of a tree branch.*

4. *After many weeks of drying, the apple faces shrivel to wizened expressions. Mrs. Steitz creates the dolls' bodies from muslin, then covers them in clothing fashioned from her great-grandmother's patterns.*

but birds and insects may feed on them if they are left unattended. Others first dry them for a day or so in an oven that is warmed only by the pilot light. In order to hasten the drying time of her apple-heads, Mrs. Steitz sometimes places them on the back window ledge of an old car that is sitting in the sun. She claims that the minimum drying time is four weeks, whatever method is used, and usually six to eight weeks are required for very thorough drying.

After the apple-head has dried for a few days, Mrs. Steitz places black-eyed peas in the eye sockets to form the eyes. As the fruit continues to shrivel, the sockets shrink around the peas, holding them in place. During the weeks of drying, she continues to modify and refine the facial features, pushing out the cheekbones, pinching in the chin, and so on. When the apple head is completely dry, she coats it with several coats of clear nail polish to protect it and further retard the natural darkening process, which does eventually turn the apple completely black.

To form the body of her dolls, she first wraps cotton batting around the stick, which by now is securely held in place by the dried apple, and then covers the batting with muslin. She then sews legs and arms, made separately of batting and muslin, onto the body of the doll. The clothing for her dolls is made by her aunt, Connie Vowels, using her great-grandmother's patterns. To finish the dolls, Mrs. Steitz glues hair on the apple heads and covers each with a bonnet.

Another doll form that has survived from colonial times is the corn-husk or corn-shuck doll, made in the same way today as in the past. Fashioned from the leaves that wrap the ear of corn as it grows, these charming dolls continue to delight children with their corn-silk hair and often elaborately layered skirts.

West Virginia corn-husk dollmaker Emma Parker prefers to use husks gathered from field-dried feed corn, but explains, "You can also shuck some eatin' ears and dry the husks in the sun. Be sure and save the silk for the hair." After separating her husks into piles based on their size, cleanliness, and quality (the best ones will go on the outside of the skirts), she soaks the dried husks until they are pliable.

Mrs. Parker forms the head first by rolling a single narrow husk from top to bottom into a log shape. She tucks in the edges as she rolls and ties a thread around

Corn-shuck dolls have been made in the South since colonial times.

Cloth dolls like this Cherokee mother and papoose accurately reflect the influence of the settlers on Indian culture.

the oblong shape to keep it from unwinding. Then she completely covers the head with another shuck that is tied at the neck to secure it and extends below the head to form the trunk of the doll. To make the arms, she pokes a hole through the trunk and pushes through a single shuck, twisted lengthwise, until it is even on both sides. Occasionally Mrs. Parker will roll the arm shuck around a piece of wire before twisting so that the arms can hold intricate positions after the doll is finished.

Clothing for the doll is also made of shucks. Diagonally crossed pieces are draped over the trunk and tied at the waist to form a blouse. Several layers of clean, unblemished shucks are then tied onto the trunk to form the skirt and are covered with a shuck sash at the waist. As the husks dry, they fluff up and out to make a secure base for the standing doll.

The final touches are added by sewing or gluing on corn silk for the hair, adding a bonnet, and making accompanying props such as baskets, cradles, or even small babies—all, of course, from additional husks.

A distinguishing characteristic of many of the corn-shuck dolls made today, including those made by Mrs. Parker, is their brightly colored clothing. In previous generations, the dolls were either left the natural color of the husks or dyed with natural dyes made from walnut hulls or butternut roots. Many dollmakers today, however, feel restricted by the seasonal nature of natural dyestuffs and are not satisfied with their muted colors, preferring the brighter hues that are possible with commercial dyes. In either case, the husks are dyed first, allowed to dry, and resoaked before they are used in the doll construction.

Rag and cloth dolls of all types originated in this country in pioneer times. These simple, soft dolls were made from scraps of material and stuffed with straw, sawdust, raw cotton, or even bran. In antebellum days,

Cradle boards hold Coushatta Indian baby dolls.

Spanish moss dolls in palmetto clothing.

(Above) *Although rag dolls similar to this Appalachian version have been made throughout the world, many people regard them as essentially American.*
(Right) *Seminole dolls made from coconut or palmetto fiber are dressed in the multi-layered fabric construction of this Southern tribe.*

Voodoo dolls are not used for harming others, as is popularly believed, but are most often employed in rituals designed to promote healing.

slave nannies often made black rag dolls for the children in the Big House.

The naive, childlike appearance of the rag doll remains appealing to children, and these traditional toys are still prevalent throughout the South. One form that is especially popular is the topsy-turvy doll, also known as double-enders or two-in-one dolls. Heads are formed at either end of a single body. The doll's long skirt conceals one end until it is turned upside down to reveal the other face. Many of the old double-enders were black and white dolls, which originated on the Southern plantations. Today the most popular characters for topsy-turvy dolls come from fairy tales such as Little Red Riding Hood.

Dolls have long been a part of Native American cultures and are still made today by many Indian women throughout the South. Cherokee dolls made in the Appalachians are clothed in long traditional skirts and often appear with babies tied to their backs in the time-honored manner. Seminole dolls, made of palmetto fiber, are also clothed in traditional dress, reflecting the cool cotton patchwork clothing of this Florida tribe. The Coushattas in Louisiana place their dolls in cradle boards made of pine needles secured with raffia. And the Houmas in Louisiana braid intricate dresses from palmetto for their Spanish moss dolls.

Dollmaking skills, like those of other traditional crafts, have been passed down from one generation to the next, and although many of the forms are found throughout the country, each region of the South boasts its own traditional styles. Whether they are braided from coarse moss grown in coastal areas or carved from tight-grained wood found in the mountains, handmade dolls possess a unique beauty and will continue, for successive generations, to provide companionship for children everywhere.

SPORTS & GAMES

The pursuit of meaningful recreational activity is not confined only to the young. For centuries adults have participated in and watched competitive games and sports ranging from the physically strenuous to the purely cerebral. For most people in recent times, however, the pursuit of leisure activity has become a complicated effort, often requiring elaborate equipment and heavy investments of time and money. In the South, however, there are folks who pursue the simpler pleasures of traditional Southern games played with handmade equipment.

Amid the limestone hills along the Kentucky-Tennessee border, devotees continue to play the century-old game of Rolley Hole marbles. Using only marbles made from the abundant flint deposits in the region, friends, families, and co-workers spend a large portion of their leisure time on marble "yards," or courts, developing their marble-shooting skills and cunning strategies.

Just before a game of Rolley Hole, players groom the three-hole court—a smooth, gravel-free, level piece of ground—by dragging an old tire across the soil, by scraping down rough spots with a board, and then

Tennessee marblemaker Bud Garrett grinds chunks of flint into perfect spheres for the game of Rolley Hole. Guaranteed for life against breakage, Mr. Garrett's marbles are highly prized.

Goingback Chiltoskey, a North Carolina Cherokee champion blowgun shooter, uses a blowgun passed down to him by his father.

sprinkling it with water to control the dust. After determining which team, or pair of players, shoots first, they begin. Alternating turns, each team traverses the yard three times, "making" each hole by "spanning," or shooting, their marbles into it, all the while trying to prevent the opposing team from doing the same by shooting their marbles away. The first team to span their marbles into all the holes on the course wins.

Commercially manufactured marbles are unsuitable for Rolley Hole because the velocity of the powerful shots would cause them to shatter. The heavier, more durable flint that is available locally has been the material of choice for generations, and handcrafted marbles are often passed down from older player to younger.

In past generations, marblemakers used a chisel and file to form a chunk of flint rock into a rough sphere, which was placed in the indentation of an abrasive

rock and left under a waterfall or in a rapidly moving creek for weeks or even months. The action of the water turned the sphere against the abrasion and wore down the rough edges, rounding it into a marble. Sudden rains or flooding, however, would wash many marbles away during this process, forcing the marblemaker to start all over.

Tennessee marblemaker and Rolley Hole player Bud Garrett solved this problem more than forty years ago by inventing a marble grinding machine that speeds up the process. He still rough cuts the flint, but then he abrades and rounds the multicolored stones by holding them against a grinding wheel until each is completely smooth and polished. Highly valued by Rolley Hole players, Mr. Garrett's marbles are guaranteed for life against breakage due to internal fissures in the stone.

Hunting is an adult pastime that has spawned a wealth of specialized equipment. Before the advent of rifles and handguns, the blowgun was used by many

Native American tribes in the South to catch wildfowl and small animals. Although they are still frighteningly lethal weapons, they are no longer used for survival hunting by the Indians, but instead for games of skill.

The blowgun is made of the same river cane that is used for basketmaking. Instead of choosing the new, tender growth as basketmakers do, gunmakers look for cane shoots that are ten to fifteen years old and up to an inch in diameter. After cutting a piece four to five feet long, they run a long hickory or metal rod through the cane to break the internal joints. Next, to smooth the inside, they bore through the cane with a piece of tin that has been repeatedly punched with a nail to make its surface abrasive. Finally, if the cane is curved or bent, they pass it through the flame of a fire to soften it, then manipulate it by hand until straight.

Although many blowgun shooters make their own guns, only a handful of people in the Indian communities have the skill to make the darts. Hayes Lossiah, a member of the North Carolina band of Cherokees, has for decades continued the traditional Cherokee method of making darts from the delicate tufts of dried thistle. He begins by collecting the dried plants, then carefully separates the wispy clusters from the seed heads.

Working with incredible speed, Mr. Lossiah attaches one tuft after another to a peeled and sharpened locust shaft by wrapping with a thin, continuous thread. As he works down the shaft, each bit of thistle overlaps the previous one in a downward spiral until he has created a five-inch-long array of thistles. To complete each dart, he burns off the top and trims straight across, forming a flat top.

Betty Dupree, director of the Cherokee crafts cooperative in North Carolina where Mr. Lossiah sells his darts, proudly states that his are among the best made. "Very few people can really do it," she explains. "Oh, they can do *at* it, but they don't do as good a job. There's just not a dart made that you can carry home after you see one of Hayes's. His are that great."

To shoot the dart, the locust shaft is first twirled between the palms of the hands to fluff out the clusters. It is then tucked into one end of the blowgun, producing an airtight fit, and aimed at the target. A puff of breath releases the dart with amazing velocity as the air forces out the layers of thistle, pushing the dart through the smooth cane.

After sharpening locust sticks, North Carolina Cherokee Hayes Lossiah skillfully wraps and layers thistle down on the shafts to create blowgun darts, completing one in less than five minutes.

Thistle darts can be lethal weapons in the hands of a practiced blowgun shooter.

STICKBALL

The ancient Native American field game of stickball, immortalized in paintings by George Catlin in the early 1800s, was the predecessor of both lacrosse and football. Although no longer played to settle disputes between villages, exhibition games of stickball are still played several times a year in various parts of the South by both the Choctaw and Cherokee tribes.

The name of the game is derived from the two ball sticks that each player uses, one held in each hand. The sticks are made from long, pliable pieces of green hickory that are cleaned of outer and inner bark and bent to form a loop at one end. After being whittled thinner, the "cup," or looped end, has six holes burned into it, and rawhide or strands of hickory bark are threaded through the holes. This latticework forms the net that will eventually catch and hold the small, walnut-sized deer-hide ball. Early Native Americans used a socket bone as the ball's core, but today's balls are filled with many assorted scraps of leather.

To begin the game, an official tosses the ball up in the midst of the game's twenty players, and immediately all twenty pairs of sticks clack together in a tangle as the players struggle to get the ball in the cups of their sticks. In the melee the ball usually falls, and the focus of the confusion quickly switches from the air to the ground.

As one player finally gains control of the ball, the others all throw their sticks aside and run to capture him as he dashes toward his goal. Other than the regulation that the sticks must be used to scoop up and hold the ball until it is six inches above the ground, there are few rules. Anything goes! There are no time-outs, no substitutions, and no time limits. Tripping, gouging, strangling, biting, and twisting the limbs of opposing team members are all part of the game. When the ball is finally thrown through the goal, the struggle begins again from the center of the field and is repeated until one side has scored twelve goals.

Ball Play of the Choctaw—Ball Up. *Oil on canvas by George Catlin, 1834-1835.*

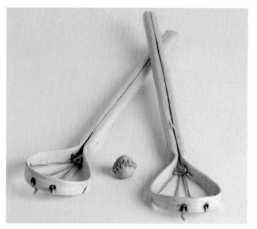

Ball sticks made from green hickory and rawhide.

Still played in exhibition games by both the Cherokee and Choctaw tribes, stickball is a fast-moving, often violent game.

FOLK TOYS & MINIATURES

Toys that move have always fascinated children. Although folk toy designs are often attributed to the mountain people of the southern Appalachians, most of them originated long before the settlement of this country and were first seen in central Europe, China, and even Egypt. Throughout the South, however, despite the influx of manufactured goods, generations of families have entertained their youngsters with toys made from mountain laurel, swamp cane, corncobs, and other readily available materials.

The Trapeze Man, also known as the Flap Jack, Rolling Clown, Jumping Jack, or Tumbling Acrobat, is one of the most popular of the articulated toys. The frame is made from two long, narrow pieces of hardwood that are joined midway by a wooden crosspiece. A jointed wooden acrobat is connected to the tops of the frame pieces by a length of string threaded through his hands. When the bottoms of the long pieces are squeezed together, the tops are pulled apart, jerking the string taut and causing the agile gymnast to flip back and forth, tirelessly performing his amazing acrobatic feats.

Another favorite is the Pecking Chickens, four carved hens attached by dowels through a wooden paddle. A string is threaded through the jointed necks of each of the chickens, dropped through a hole in the paddle, and attached to a single weight, usually a wooden ball or piece of corncob that hangs below the paddle. As the paddle is swung around and around in a

The Flap Jack, a popular folk toy in the South for generations, tirelessly flips back and forth as the wooden handles are squeezed together.

horizontal plane, the weight swings in a circular motion, jerking down the chickens' counterweighted heads in succession to peck at pieces of corn glued to the paddle top.

The appeal of some toys resides in their ability to mystify. Jacob's Ladder, also known as Clatter Blocks and Tumbling Squares, is one such example. A series of flat wooden blocks connected to one another by narrow strips of cloth, this simple toy has been perplexing children for generations. When the top block is grasped between the thumb and forefinger and tipped to touch the next block, the blocks all appear to tumble down but, mysteriously, do not come apart. If a dollar bill is folded and placed under the cloth strips of one of the blocks, it will disappear and then magically reappear as the blocks tumble, further mystifying the viewer.

Another bewildering amusement, simply whittled from a few small branches, is the Gee Haw Whimmy Diddle, also known as a Ziggerboo, a Jeepstick, or a Hoodoo Stick. A tree branch six to eight inches long is whittled down to bare wood and then nicked near one end with six to eight closely placed notches. A small, propeller-shaped piece is whittled from another branch and loosely attached with a pin or small nail perpendicular to the notched end of the larger stick, where it will spin easily. A third branch, about four inches in length, is whittled simply for use as a rubbing stick.

The object of the Whimmy Diddle is to rub the smaller stick over the notches to make the propeller spin and then mysteriously change the direction of the propeller, apparently by the command of "Gee!" or "Haw!," exclamations commonly used to command a team of mules or horses to turn right or left. To operate the toy, the notched stick is held lightly in one hand, with the index finger laid along the side of the stick.

The sounds of farm and field are magically recreated with these two toys, as the wooden chickens peck at their feed and the horse's hooves clack in sequence against a platform.

Two of the author's children try to hook the corncob ball on the ring of their Flipperdingers by floating them on a steady stream of air.

The rubbing stick is held in the other hand and briskly rubbed back and forth over the notches on the larger stick. The resulting vibrations cause the propeller to spin. To change the propeller's direction, the index finger is retracted, the thumb laid along the other side of the stick, and the notches rubbed again.

The Whimmy Diddle has proved to be such a popular folk toy that it was offered as a Bicentennial premium by the Quaker Oats Company and has even spawned its own Annual World Gee Haw Whimmy Diddle Competition held in North Carolina. There are three classes of competitors—those under twelve years old, those older than twelve and not a previous winner, and the professionals (previous winners and those who feel that their experience merits inclusion in this class). After beginning with warm-up trials, the contestants compete for prizes in the Most Unusual Whimmy Diddle and the World Competition contests. Not only are there contests to measure skill, but also demonstrations are given showing how to whittle Whimmy Diddles from native woods.

Some folk toys require a degree of skill to work properly, such as the Flipperdinger, a seemingly simple toy made from a piece of swamp cane or reed. The interior of the cane is reamed out except for the internal joint on one end, which acts as a plug. A hole is bored into the top of the cane near the plugged joint, and a smaller piece of hollowed reed is inserted into the hole as the air nozzle. In front of the nozzle, an elevated ring (like a tiny basketball hoop) is attached to the larger piece of cane. Finally, a featherweight ball is carved from the pith at the center of a cornstalk, pierced with a hooked piece of wire, and placed squarely on the nozzle.

The challenge is to blow steadily and gently through the larger cane, making the ball rise and, with skill, hooking it on the wire hoop above. More difficult is the trick of blowing and *un*hooking the ball from the hoop, bringing it down to settle once again on the nozzle.

The actions of many of these old folk toys illustrate some basic principles of physics. The tendency of a ball to remain balanced on a stream of air, as demonstrated by the Flipperdinger, was proclaimed in the 1700s as Bernoulli's Principle. A more complex explanation of how the Whimmy Diddle works is offered by West Virginia toymaker Dick Schnacke: "The variably generated vibration frequencies and harmonics thereof react in concert upon the main body of a given mass and configuration, to set up vibration patterns and notes which agitate the essentially statically balanced and frictionless rotor into rhythmic rotational movement. Understand?"

The scientific principles may or may not be understood, but to the amazed child or amused adult, the twirling of a propeller, the flipping of an acrobat, or the levitation of a ball is pure and simple magic.

A tiny doll's rocker drawn up to the fire along with the family's chairs; a flotilla of small boats to sail in a creek; or a horse-drawn wagon reminiscent of the one that brought an early family to its homestead—such diminutive counterparts to the full-scale adult world have long existed as touching reminders of the child's life within a family. Although most early miniatures were made by parents, sometimes doll furniture was ordered from a local cabinetmaker along with the family's table or hutch, and occasionally a salesman's miniature sample would make its way into the hands of a child.

Miniatures are still made today by inventive and resourceful craftspeople throughout the South. Based on designs passed down within a family or community or simply remembered from days gone by, these toys often provide an important glimpse into the world of past generations.

Doll furniture, always a small-scale favorite, is most often produced today in mountain areas abundant in hardwoods. Tennessean Robert Tate begins his doll chairs and loveseats by cutting his own oak, walnut, maple, cherry, and poplar from the hills surrounding his home in Cannon County. Following the traditional method of chairmaking, he uses no nails to construct his furniture. Instead, he relies on the shrinkage of the wood to hold the parts together. "The pieces are just driven together," he explains. "When

Robert Tate creates thousands of pieces of doll furniture each year from the wooded hills surrounding his Cannon County, Tennessee, home.

that green post finishes drying, it tightens up on that dowel."

After the chair frames are made and dried, they are "bottomed" by his son, his daughter-in-law, and his two grandsons. Using a paper product they call cane bottom, they wrap and weave the flat material around the top rungs of the chair, making a strong, flexible seat in exactly the same way as their neighbors who make full-scale versions of these chairs do.

North Carolina toymaker Willard Watson boasts that his "baby doll beds are some of the prettiest things you'll ever look at yet." Also working with a variety of woods, including curly maple, black walnut, and black cherry, he prefers wild cherry because of the beauty of its surface when finished. The beds, accurate reproductions of four-poster slat beds, are furnished with foam rubber mattresses and pillows. Mr. Watson's wife, Ora, an accomplished quiltmaker, occasionally makes a miniature quilt for the beds, using patterns from quilts on her family's beds.

Drawing on memories of pre-mechanized mountain farm life, Mr. Watson also makes a wonderful variety of

North Carolina toymaker Willard Watson creates some of the most attractive doll beds.

Mr. Tate's small-scale furniture is constructed with no nails. He relies instead on the traditional method of shrinking of green wood around dry.

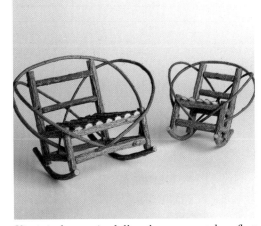

Virginia bent-twig doll rockers accurately reflect another popular type of Southern chair construction.

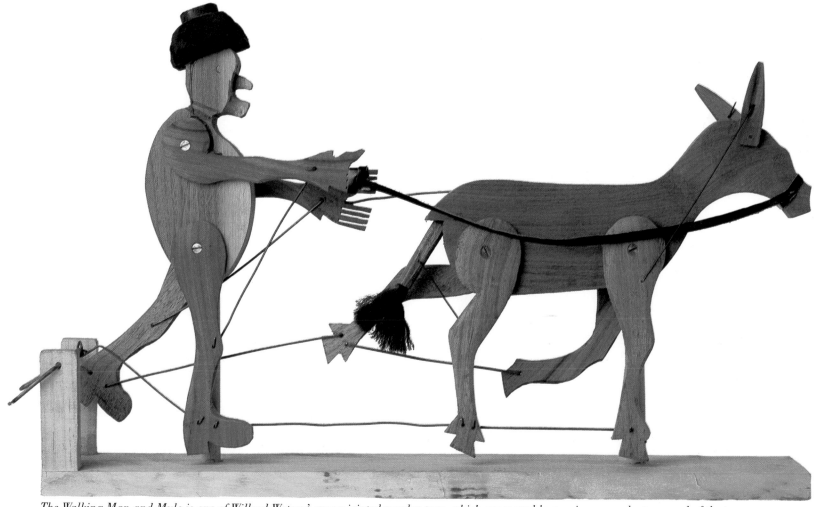

The Walking Man and Mule is one of Willard Watson's many jointed wooden toys, which are moved by turning a crank at one end of the toy.

farm sleds, wagons, and carriages. "They used sleds in the mountain sections all the time," he recalls, "and they did as far back as I can remember. I've helped make big sleds for the farm. We'd go to the woods and hew the runners out of sourwood with an ax." Now his miniature wooden sleds and wagons are driven by little wooden men clothed in overalls sewn by his daughter and are pulled by wooden mules connected to the conveyances with tiny metal chains threaded through leather harnesses. Many of the wagons and sleds carry tiny hoes, rakes, and hand plows, accurate reproduc-

tions of farm implements from past generations.

Some of his carved wooden toys are jointed, their limbs intricately connected to one another by threads and wires, and are moved by the turn of a crank or handle at one end. One model shows a man walking behind a mule, the feet of both propelled by the movement of a crank. Another farmer and animal toy, called the Bouncing Pig, is also run by a crank. As the handle of this toy is turned, the hickory rod held in the man's hand moves up and down behind the pig in a rapid, whipping motion. And each time the hickory

Meticulous reproductions of horse-drawn stagecoaches, reminiscent of those that served early American life, are still made today by Southern craftsmen.

Many mountain toymakers like Willard Watson draw upon memories of farm life before mechanization, when mule-driven wagons were commonly used.

stick comes down, the pig's hindquarters kick straight up into the air.

Like many toymakers, Mr. Watson does not work from patterns but relies on his own memories to direct his work. "When I find a piece of wood I like, I just take it to bed with me," he explains, "and look at it. Then I go down the next day and make the toy. And I can't hardly tell you how long it takes me to make a toy either. I work on it 'til I get tired of it, then I lay it down and pick up another piece and work on *it*."

Along the coastal areas of the South, where fishing remains an integral part of life, toy boats abound. In some coastal communities, these toys are a tangible remnant of historic forms abandoned long ago by full-scale boat builders but retained in the vivid memories of elderly toymakers.

One such boat is the dugout pirogue, which was common in southwest Louisiana before the turn of the century but is now made only in toy form. Long before the area was settled by the French, Native Americans split huge cypress logs in half, burned their interiors, and then dug out the burned wood to form pod-shaped vessels for transportation on the narrow swamps. As the area became settled and the cypress forests were decimated by the lumber industry, the dugouts were replaced by boats constructed from planks of other types of wood. Today, as the last remaining pieces of old cypress float ashore in the form of driftwood, they are collected and lovingly carved into small versions of the dugout pirogue.

Along with the nostalgic feelings evoked by these small-scale reproductions comes the bittersweet recognition that they may be the last remaining artifacts of ways of life now vanished. The craft of these toymakers connects us to a time replaced by new technologies, to a history that has, in many cases, been otherwise forgotten.

Dugout pirogues are now made only in toy form by Louisiana craftsmen like Antoine Billiot.

Cyril Billiot's toy plank pirogues, from his coastal community in Terrebonne Parish, Louisiana, trace their ancestry back to vessels made by the area's early native tribes.

WOODWORKING

Many traditional instruments, including the double dulcimer, continue to be produced by hand throughout the South.

In the settling of a new country, few things are so important as the ability to work with what is at hand. More than any other material, wood was the most available material for the early American settlers. The numerous forests throughout the South provided abundant resources for those who were forging their lives in a wilderness. These marvelous forests represented one of the miracles of the New World.

But wood is not a single material that can be easily understood. There are a great many species—some native only to a limited region—and each has its own distinct qualities. Wood craftsmen understood the differences of color, grain, hardness, pliability, workability, resilience, and resistance to weather or insects, and exploited the unique qualities of each material. Similar objects made of different kinds of wood reveal very different qualities. Moreover, different woods inspired divergent kinds of objects. The variety is vast.

As settlers moved into the frontier, when things made from iron were often too hard to come by or too expensive, wood performed many of the functions that we now identify with metals. Long before nails were commonly available in large quantities, home builders joined logs together with mortise and tenon, dovetail, and similar joints, and cabinetmakers and chairmakers relied on the shrinkage of green wood around dry wood to join together pieces of furniture. "Tight coopers," who made containers for liquids, and "slack coopers," who made containers for solids, often bound their hand-hewn staves with hickory bark hoops until the introduction of iron ones. Turners produced treenware, which was the churns, bowls, and spoons required for kitchen use. Millwrights created the gears, wheels, and shafts for the mills that ground their grain, and wainwrights produced the carriages and wagons that were used to transport the goods to market.

The woodcrafter's intimate understanding of woods has naturally been lost as new materials and more mechanized means of production have taken over. However, a few woodworking traditions have been maintained from place to place across the South. The craft traditions in woodworking are rich and varied.

For the most part, the surviving craft forms have served a purpose that cannot be served by alternative forms. Handcrafted musical instruments, for example—dulcimers, fiddles, mandolins, accordions, and fifes—are prized by musicians because of the remarkable attention to detail that goes into their construction and because of the acoustical rewards of the wood. And who can measure the aesthetic appeal of playing Appalachian folk tunes on an instrument made from Appalachian wood by an Appalachian craftsperson?

Similarly, the boats made locally for a cash-poor hunting and fishing culture in southern Louisiana cannot be more efficiently replaced by an affordable manufactured vessel. Nor can factory-made furniture beat the quality and cost of chairs made by mountain craftsmen in North Carolina or Tennessee. And the multitude of bird houses have all survived in response to a combination of economic, functional, and aesthetic requirements not otherwise matched.

But whatever the object made and however well served its function, to both craftsperson and observer, working imaginatively and economically with the bounty of one's own land is a sheer sensory delight. The variety of woods, the tactile qualities and the responsiveness of the material, the satisfaction of refining the wood and shaping it into something functional and handsome, still attract woodworkers, and the traditions continue.

DULCIMERS

The mountain dulcimer is one of the oldest instruments in the United States and, like the banjo, is a unique indigenous form. It originated in the Appalachians and, until recently, was made only there. Like many other craft forms, the dulcimer derived from European folk forms familiar to the immigrants who settled in the mountain areas of the South. The Swedish *hummel*, the Norwegian *langelaik*, and the German *sheitholt* are among its ancestors. While the shapes of the instruments differed from culture to culture, the principle was the same: several strings stretched across an elongated hollow wooden box were plucked, or "swept," with the fingers or a pick to produce sound.

Easily constructed, lightweight and therefore portable, the mountain or Appalachian dulcimer (also known as the lap or plucked dulcimer or dulcymore) has enjoyed a popularity for generations. Deriving its name from the Latin and Greek words for "sweet song," the dulcimer has accompanied many mountain songfests with its soft, haunting tones.

Because it is played sitting down, it has evolved as an instrument for use at quiet, intimate occasions, usually to accompany a single voice. With the introduction of the guitar in the first part of the twentieth century, however, and the subsequent emergence of the amplified string band, the quiet sound of the solo dulcimer could not compete. Had it not been for the folk music revival of the late 1950s, the dulcimer might have vanished entirely as an instrument in use.

Today, however, dulcimer makers throughout the South are producing the narrow-bodied instruments by hand. Although made in several different shapes, including teardrop, waspwaist, and hourglass, the

Uncle Ed Thomas, Dulcimer Maker, *ca. 1930*.

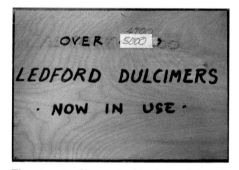

The sign in Homer Ledford's workshop is frequently updated.

Kentuckian Warren May's dulcimers often make use of natural knots in the wood as the instruments' sound holes.

basic elongated configuration of several strings stretched along the top of a narrow, hollow box has not changed for centuries.

Perhaps the most distinct difference from one dulcimer to another is the type of wood used in its construction, a decision that is usually based on what is available locally. Because the sound of the instrument is produced by the vibrations of plucked or strummed strings resonating in the hollow chamber of the box, the density of the wood used in its construction greatly affects the sound.

Kentuckian Warren May, a craftsman who makes dulcimers, explains: "Light woods like poplar have a resonant, loud sound. Tougher woods like walnut have a smooth, mellow voice. Cherry is smooth but substantially brighter, because the wood is harder. And maple produces very soft, clear tones."

Mr. May begins by cutting the pieces of the dulcimer from visually similar pieces of a single species of wood. "Even though the pieces may come out of different boards, there are usually coordinating graining patterns in each." He shapes the sides by first

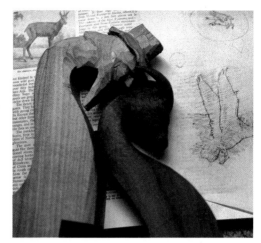

The designs of Homer Ledford's scroll tops vary widely, many taken from old engravings.

A carved duck's head, a favorite of Mr. Ledford and his customers, sits atop a walnut dulcimer.

Warren May shapes the sides of his dulcimers by bending previously soaked wood strips to fit in a pegged mold. When dry, they will retain their shapes.

soaking them in a long tray of water, then forming them in molds made from nails tapped into resurrected old log cabin floorboards. When dry, the sides retain their curves, allowing him to glue them to the shaped top and back of the instrument. The long fretboard is glued onto the top, the metal frets are added, and the dulcimer is sanded and varnished.

Homer Ledford, also from Kentucky, combines different types of wood in his dulcimers. For his tops, he prefers a softwood like spruce or poplar to ensure a clear, bright sound, and often uses walnut for the back

and sides. Mr. Ledford, who has made more than 5,000 dulcimers in the past forty years, also adjusts the size of the sound holes from one instrument to the next to vary the sound. "When small holes are used and the dulcimer is enclosed more," he explains, "the air vibrates slower, making a bass sound. When it vibrates faster, as with the larger holes, you get a treble sound."

Although the size of the sound holes can considerably change the tone of the instrument, the shape of the holes is a purely decorative element. Ranging from simple, round openings to elaborately carved flowers,

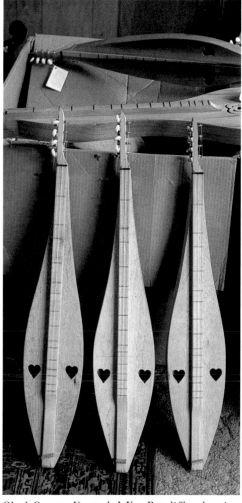

J. C. Ramey of Grayson County, Kentucky, taps the metal fret pieces into the neck of a dulcimer. He will then complete its construction by gluing the neck to the top.

Clark County, Kentucky's Ken Ratcliff makes simple dulcimers for use in the region's schools.

the style of every person who makes dulcimers is distinguishing and often becomes a means of identifying the instruments. A common motif has been the heart shape, often carved upside down. As the legend goes, the heart that is turned from bottom to top will not bleed and symbolizes steadfast devotion.

Regardless of the shape or the kind of wood, mountain dulcimers are relatively easy to play. The instrument is placed on the player's lap with the scroll, or neck, to the left. The left hand presses down the strings along the fretboard either with the fingers or with a small wooden "noter," and the right hand sweeps or plucks the strings with a quill, a guitar pick, or fingertips. Because the frets are tuned to a standard diatonic, eight-toned scale, picking out a tune is as easy as playing the white keys of a piano.

Although not quite as easy to play as the mountain dulcimer, the hammered dulcimer, whose origins go back to Biblical times, has also remained a popular instrument in the South. Hammered dulcimers, typically supported on special stands, usually have trapezoidal-shaped, shallow boxes, with forty-eight strings

North Carolina instrument maker Jim Trantham carves a dogwood blossom into the scroll . . .

and creates sound holes by delicately carving the native flower into the dulcimer's top.

Kentuckian Blake Barker strikes out a tune with maple hammers on his trapezoidal-shaped hammered dulcimer, made from mahogany, maple, and redwood.

stretched tautly over two bridges, or supports, above the wooden top. The strings are not swept with the fingers as mountain dulcimers are, but are struck with hammers, usually thin handled sticks (ranging from corset stays to elegantly carved rosewood) often topped by padded knobs of leather or felt.

Although heavier and far less portable than the mountain variety, the hammered dulcimer, which has more than ten times the number of strings and is tuned to include both sharp and flat notes, is capable of a greater range of sounds. It also sustains the sounds of the hammered strings, like the harp. When the strings are struck in rapid succession, the dulcimer seems to accompany itself, as the sounds of the previously played notes mingle with the new ones.

In form, in craftsmanship, in materials and sound, all dulcimers—regardless of their construction or their playing—somehow speak to a love of simplicity, to the careful choices and heartfelt standards that make a thing belong, ineffably, to its place and its people.

(Right) J. C. Ramey tunes his completed dulcimer. His sound hole design, called "kissing hearts," is a hallmark identifying his instruments.

MANDOLINS & FIDDLES

The violin, or fiddle as it is known to folk musicians throughout the South, has for generations been the preeminent instrument for entertaining at community social gatherings. Developed in Europe in the 1600s, it was brought to America by the settlers of many cultures, from the Cajuns of Louisiana to the Scotch-Irish of the Appalachians.

The mandolin, although as thoroughly pedigreed as the fiddle, has enjoyed its current popularity as a folk instrument in Southern performance ensembles for less than half a century. A member of the lute family, with its sets of double strings, the early mandolin was gourd-backed and often called a "tater bug" because its bulbous shape and striped back so closely resembled the insect. The flat backs of recent models make them

Although popular as a folk instrument in Southern performance groups for only half a century, the mandolin continues to be an instrument found in all traditional bluegrass bands.

Fiddles, on the other hand, have for generations been the principal instrument in country bands.

easier to play when standing up. Although most of today's fiddles and mandolins are factory manufactured, a few craftspeople in the South continue the laborious tradition of producing one-of-a-kind instruments by hand.

Seemingly quite different from each other, the mandolin and the fiddle are actually closely related, both in form and in context. They are tuned exactly alike and constructed with similar woods. Each employs a spruce top for resonance, and will often have highly figured grains on the back and sides for visual effect.

Along with the fiddle, as well as the guitar, bass, and five-string banjo, the mandolin has been integral to the traditional bluegrass band since Bill Monroe introduced the instrument as part of his Bluegrass Boys band in the 1930s.

LIMBERJACK

One object frequently seen at musical gatherings is not a musical instrument at all, but a small rhythm doll with jointed arms and legs. The Limberjack, also known as a Stomper Doll or Dancing Doll, has been used for generations to amuse children while developing their sense of rhythm at the same time.

The Limberjack's head and torso are usually cut from a single piece of wood, while its arms, lower legs, and upper legs are separately made and loosely jointed together with small nails or wooden pegs. A shallow hole is drilled into its back and a dowel inserted that, when held, suspends the doll over a thin, narrow board or paddle about twenty inches long.

To make the Limberjack dance, a child sits on a chair or stool and braces about one-third of the paddle under his or her thigh, allowing the rest to protrude from the chair. The dowel is secured firmly into the hole in the Limberjack's back, and the doll held over the far end of the paddle, with its feet barely touching the "dance floor." As a lively tune is played, the child taps on the paddle behind the doll in time to the music, making it bounce up and down. As the paddle hits its feet, with a delightful sound the doll will begin jumping and tapping a realistic dance along the paddle, its movements varied by the force and tempo of the tapping. With a little practice, the Limberjack can be made to swing its arms, do the splits, and even bow at the end of the song!

Limberjacks are made from separate pieces of wood, loosely jointed together.

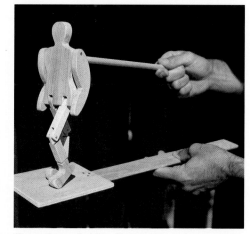

Kentuckian Debbie Von Bokern demonstrates her limberjack, causing it to dance and kick.

ACCORDIONS

With beer, *boudin* sausage, and music, renowned accordion craftsman Marc Savoy and his friends celebrate their rich Cajun heritage each Saturday morning in his shop in Eunice, Louisiana. Mr. Savoy's passion is the preservation of his inherited musical tradition, one that has, amid the cultural blendings of America, remained uniquely intact since the arrival of the first Acadian settlers in mid-eighteenth-century Louisiana.

At the heart of this traditional sound is the distinct bawling voice of the Cajun accordion. Although the fiddle was the first instrument of choice among the French immigrants, the accordion has gradually surpassed it in popularity over the last fifty years. Originally imported from Germany, almost all accordions played today by Cajun musicians are handbuilt by one of nearly forty local craftspeople, virtually all of them taught, or at least inspired, by Marc Savoy.

Working in the back of his store, often among the company of a changing variety of local musicians who drop in, Mr. Savoy devotes himself to the careful handcrafting of nearly sixty accordions each year, five or six of them under construction at any given time. Each accordion begins as an airtight box, which he builds from hardwood such as Louisiana sweet gum, curly maple, or ebony. The woods are selected for their density, required to sustain and temper the sound.

As Mr. Savoy tells it, the ascendancy of the accordion over the fiddle derives, in part, from its power to be heard over the boisterous sounds of a Cajun dance hall. "The Cajuns are not known to be very quiet people," he says. "So you can imagine back in the 1800s, when you were playing a house party with a fiddle, you didn't have much volume with a bunch of unruly Cajuns around. Have you ever heard an accordion? You can blow the windows out!" There is a sort of happy violence to its playing, as the cloth and sheepskin bellows are rhythmically expanded and contracted, infusing the box with air as it is drawn in and expelled across the steel reeds.

Fine reeds, capable of reacting quickly to the move-

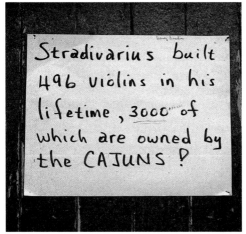

This sign greets customers in Marc Savoy's Louisiana music store.

Mr. Savoy relaxes with one of his instruments on the porch swing of his Louisiana home.

Elton Quebedeaux, one of nearly forty local accordion makers inspired by the work of Marc Savoy, creates these diminutive Cajun accordions in a workshop attached to his Louisiana home.

ment of air from the bellows, and a well-built box are the components of a superior accordion. "I try to build into my instruments a real fast response," Mr. Savoy explains. "My objective is to inject a bright, clear tone with a minimum of movement. A good musician, working with a good instrument, won't have to move his bellows much. If you see somebody stretching his bellows all over the place, either he has a terrible accordion or he can't play it."

Unlike the larger, heavier, piano-style accordions with their rows of black and white keys tuned to a fully chromatic scale, the more diminutive German-style Cajun accordion, equipped with only ten buttons instead of many keys, is tuned to a simpler, eight-tone scale, the sound varied by the pushing and pulling on the bellows. Speaking of its limitations, Cajun musician Zachary Richard, who uses two of Savoy's accordions, says, "It's just a big harmonica is all it is."

It is both an instrument for making music and a centerpiece of the rollicking Cajun social life. In Marc Savoy's words, "You can step on it, walk on it, leave it out in the rain, and you can still play on it."

FIFES

Afro-American communities in the deep South have always maintained their own musical traditions, some of which vary little from the forms brought to this country by the first West African slaves a few hundred years ago. One such tradition is found among a few Mississippi Delta families whose music combines the melodic playing of a simple cane fife with a rhythmic complexity of drums firmly rooted in an African heritage.

Mississippian Othar Turner started making fifes and "blowing the cane" more than six decades ago, at the age of thirteen. Today, with his daughter playing lead snare and bass drum and two friends also on bass drums, his Rising Star Fife and Drum Band entertains delighted audiences, from backyard barbecues to crowded festivals, with the traditional tunes of his youth.

To begin a fife, Mr. Turner cuts a straight piece of swamp cane or bamboo about a foot long and an inch in diameter. He heats a long metal rod until red-hot in a fire he has made in an open-topped metal can. Protecting his hands with a heavy piece of cloth, he removes the rod from the fire and carefully inserts its tip in the end of the cane, slowly twisting it as it burns through the length of the cane to create an even, hollow bore.

Next, he determines where the mouth and finger holes should go by holding the cane up to his mouth flute-style, then marking their correct placement with the tip of his pocketknife. Heating the metal once again, he uses the tip of the rod to burn through the top of the cane at the marked places, taking care not to bore through to the other side. When all the holes have been pierced and the rough edges sanded smooth, the instrument is ready to play.

Now in his late seventies, Mr. Turner is the only remaining fifemaker and player in his Mississippi community. Concerned for her father and for the demise of these musical traditions, his daughter Bernice says, "Daddy's the only one. If somethin' happens to Daddy, the music will die out."

1. Othar Turner first bores through cane.

3. *He then burns through the top of the cane with the hot poker where he has marked.*

2. *After breaking the internal joints of the cane with a red-hot poker, Mr. Turner marks the correct placement of the mouth and finger holes with the tip of his knife.*

4. *When all the holes have been burned into the cane, it is ready to play.*

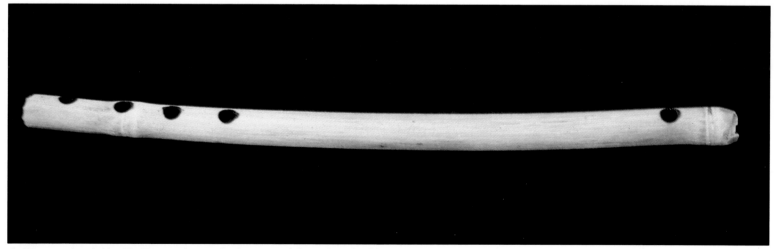

5. *The completed fife. Mr. Turner plays at barbecues and festivals in his Mississippi community and throughout the South.*

CHAIRS

Peter Ingram, Chairmaker. Berea, Kentucky, *ca.1934,*
by Doris Ulmann.

The familiar mountain-style "settin'" chair, also known as a ladder-back, split-back, split-bottom, or mule-ear chair for its tapered, pointed finials, remains among the most popular craft items still extensively hand produced throughout the South. Whereas a table would typically require sophisticated and expensive joining and planing equipment, a handsome, stout, and comfortable traditional chair can be easily assembled with only a simple lathe, drill, and carpenter's tools.

In Cannon County, Tennessee, the chairmaker's craft has continued and thrived as a cottage industry, as has basketmaking. Just about everyone there either turns trees into chairs or baskets or has a relative who does. J. Paul Newby, a lifetime area resident, explains:

"This was their money crop, and a pretty good one at that. It was a medium of exchange for them. People in adjoining states quit these crafts when prosperity came. They went on to bigger cities, and so on. But Cannon County had a lot of people whose children and grandchildren wanted to stay around in their little country towns. So they learned the art. They've held onto it, and done it for a living."

Ronnie Smith began learning chairmaking from his granddad at the age of ten, when he had to stand up on a piece of timber to work the lathe. Working with two assistants in a small shop redolent with the wet, fragrant smell of freshly milled timber, he now makes nearly forty chairs each week. The straight, strong backs, the gently curved, slatted seats, and the lines of

Tennessee chairmaker Ronnie Smith works at his lathe, turning the posts and rounds for the forty chairs he makes each week.

armrests and finials have changed little from his grandfather's designs.

Although he used to lumber his own wood when he was a boy, he now purchases the raw stock from a local timber mill. "I have them slice the wood in three thicknesses," he explains, "and they just saw it log-wide that-a-way, and leave the bark on it and everything. We cut it all up, turn all the posts, and, of course, we have to saw all the backs, slats, runners, and arms. We mark every one of 'em one at a time, and saw 'em one at a time."

Regardless of its beauty, a chair is only as good as its joints. To ensure a solid piece of furniture, Mr. Smith does not use nails, which can loosen and fall out over time. He relies, instead, on the traditional method of using green, or undried, lumber for the posts so that they will tighten as they dry around the seasoned rungs, or "rounds." "All you do is bore all the holes in the green tree wood and drive the chair rounds in. If you don't drive the chair rounds in the holes today, why, it's gonna be real hard to drive 'em in tomorrow. The wood will dry up overnight from the heat of the stove." As the posts dry around the carefully fitted rounds, the joints are locked tightly into a secure fit.

A half-dozen different hardwoods are used for his chairs, depending on what is seasonally available at the mill. He prefers ash because of its straight grain and limited tendency to split, but there is a handle factory near him that buys most of his region's ash at prices that he can't afford. Many people request maple because of its even, closed grain, which takes stain well, and that suits him just fine. "Oak will sand better and saw better than maple, but I believe I'd rather turn a maple post than an oak post. The shavin's come off the oak so fine, seems like they just stick to you, and stick to your shirt, and just beat you to death."

When the chairs are finished, Ronnie Smith takes

General Ponder cuts enough black willow at one time for several chairs.

When completed, Mr. Smith's chairs are stored in the loft of his barn to await buyers. Many people request chairs made from maple, but he will turn a chair from whatever wood is available.

General Ponder's settee has the graceful arches characteristic of willow furniture.

them to a loft area above his shop to await a buyer. Occasionally he sits at a local gas station with a few of them, waiting for customers, but most are sold to people who somehow, through word of mouth or by happy coincidence, find his shop along the back roads.

Another popular wood used for furniture making throughout the South is the strong yet extremely flexible black willow, cousin to the weeping variety, which grows along lakes and rivers. Whole young saplings and long branches from older trees are fashioned into graceful chairs and settees with qualities both rustic and delicate. Sometimes the bark is left on, providing a natural shield against the weather and making the chairs suitable for outdoor use.

Texas chairmaker General Ponder first learned to work with willow as a young boy in the early 1930s in Milam County, Texas. He was sitting on the porch with a neighbor who had a willow chair that was in need of repair. She mentioned to him that she was anxious for the chair man to come fix it for her. "I told her I'd fix it," he recalls. "She said, 'Boy, you know you can't fix no chair,' and I said, 'I can *make* a chair.' I got off the porch and went on out to the woods. I already knowed how to cut the wood and everything. All I had to do was to look at how the chair was made and start out and make one like it. That first day I went out, I brought back a big old double chair! That first chair I made, it was pretty, but it wasn't too stout. Later on, I learned from the older chairmakers how to station them to be on a stout foundation."

Today, after half a century, he continues to cut willow along the river near his home. After harvesting enough for two or three chairs, he lets the wood dry, then trims off the leaves and small branches. Carefully bending the pieces into graceful arcs, he nails them together one by one to create the broad fanning planes of the arms and backs. Modest about his creations, he simply states, "You just cut the wood, and then you trim it down and make 'em. That's about the size of it."

Some ladder-backs, rockers, and other handcrafted chairs are not made with wooden seats, but have bottoms woven from whatever materials are handy—bark strips, baling twine, antenna wire, or even twisted or plaited corn shucks! Ronnie Smith's mother, Nadine Smith, uses a rolled paper product, commonly called rush, to bottom some of Mr. Smith's chairs. With flying fingers, she can bottom a dining room chair in thirty minutes, producing a strong, attractive, double-thick seat that she stains or coats with clear varnish to complete.

Long splits of white oak and the inner bark from a hickory tree are often used for seating in mountain areas where the material is plentiful. Of the two, hickory is preferred because it doesn't snap and split when weight is placed directly on it. To harvest the bark, a small hickory sapling about six to eight inches in diameter is cut down, and the straight trunk, or "pole," is sawed off just below the first branch. Its outer bark is carefully shaved off with a knife, leaving the tough, leathery inner bark attached. With the tip of

Corn Husk Chair Seats *by Doris Ulmann, ca. 1930.*

Ronnie Smith's mother, Nadine, bottoms many of his chairs with a rolled paper called rush.

The tough, inner bark of the hickory tree provides an especially stout chair bottom.

Corn husks continue to be a sturdy and useful material for bottoming chairs.

Long, thin splits of white oak are often used in mountain regions where the material is plentiful.

Many chairmakers still use the traditional cane to back and bottom their furniture.

the knife, the inner bark is scored into strips about one inch wide running the entire length of the pole. At the bottom of the tree, the edge of one scored strip is lifted with the tip of the knife and grasped between the thumb and forefinger. In one swift movement, the strip is peeled from the pole with a sharp snap! The process is repeated until the entire tree has been stripped. If the strips are especially thick, they can be peeled to double the harvest. If left to dry, they can be soaked in water to restore their pliability.

The actual bottoming pattern may vary slightly from chair to chair, but the basic technique is the same. The seating material is wrapped from front to back around the top rungs, keeping the individual strips tight against one another. Spanning between the side rungs, strips are then woven across, over, and under the previously wrapped strips, resulting in a handsome, comfortable, and durable twill.

The techniques for making hardwood and willow chairs differ little from place to place, but to even the most casual observer, the extraordinary variety of patterns, shapes, and details is delightfully apparent.

BOATS

While the vast frontiers of the new American territories were being settled by waves of immigrants in Conestoga wagons, the sprawling coastal region along the continent's oceans, rivers, lakes, and swamps were being approached by boat. Small watercraft, handmade by their users or by local boat builders following traditional patterns, have for centuries continued in use along the many water-bound communities throughout the South.

Vessels of many types, from flat-bottomed boats for inland marshes and swamps to deep-keeled trawlers for ocean fishing, are made according to designs that are often unique to their localities. In southern Louisiana, for instance, where a life of economic subsistence continues along narrow swamps and bayous, the favored watercraft has, for centuries, been the pirogue. A flat-bottomed, narrow boat pointed on both ends, the pirogue (pronounced "pee-row," a Carib Indian word meaning "dugout") traces its ancestry back to very similar vessels made from hollowed-out logs by the area's early native tribes.

After felling a cypress tree with fire, the Indians burned the log along its length, padding it with clay around the bottom and ends to prevent the fire from burning through. As the wood was charred by the fire, it was scraped out until the log was hollow. The French who settled in Louisiana used tools to refine the process—the ax for cutting down the trees and roughly shaping the logs, and the curved-bladed adz for hollowing them out.

Over the years the pirogue changed in size and use. The earliest, large ones were used to haul heavy cargos of people and goods, but their weight and size made them difficult to portage. The smaller one- or two-person dugout pirogues remained popular until the early 1900s when most of Louisiana's virgin cypress timber was decimated by the lumber industry. "Every big tree in the Atchafaylaya Basin that wasn't hollow was cut down," explains lifelong resident Greg Guirard. "By the late 1920s they were all gone. This young cypress, it's very lightweight and soft. The old

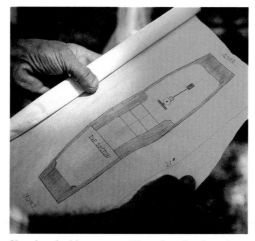

Handcrafted boats are still produced today along the many waterbound communities in the South.

Louisiana boat builder Raymond Sedotal and his friends construct a plank pirogue at the Festival of American Folklife in Washington, D.C.

cypress was very oily and very heavy. Solid. If you made a dugout out from today's cypress, it would bust very easily."

Modern pirogues are built from planks of wood or even of marine plywood. Based on the form and design of the old dugouts, the "plank" pirogue remains an ideal boat for hunting, trapping, and fishing in the characteristic shallows of the bayou. Typically built to fit a single person, it is usually no wider than two feet and only a foot deep. With only two or three planks used for the bottom and a single plank for each side, the plank pirogue requires limited caulking or additional structure. Its flat bottom and sharply tapered bow and stern allow it to be easily navigated where no other type of boat can go. "When the water goes down in the springtime," Mr. Guirard explains, "fishermen who normally use a 50 or 80 horsepower motor often have to turn to pirogues in order to get back to where the crawfish are. The water may only be four inches deep in some parts. You get through that kind of water with a pirogue."

Low-hanging tree limbs, often draped with long wisps of Spanish moss, as well as cypress "knees," the remaining stumps of trees lumbered long ago and hidden beneath the water, require that pirogues be maneuvered with paddles rather than broad-sweeping oars. Because cypress is still the wood of choice, boatmakers, whenever possible, carve their T-shaped paddles from seasoned pickets of old cypress fences.

Fourches, or long push poles, are often used to propel the boats in very shallow, marshy water. Made from a variety of materials, including bamboo, tree branches, and old cypress, they are forked at the submerged end to prevent the pole from sinking into the silty bottoms.

The pirogue and other traditional boats such as the skiff, bateau, and flatboat, continue to be crafted in the

South because of their critical roles in local economies. Working in backyards and garages, people whose existence depends upon the water have found that adherence to the time-tested shapes and forms of boats is an effective strategy for keeping their style of life viable throughout the generations.

Woodworker Eddy Greig specializes in building pirogues such as this one made in the shop near his home in St. Martin Parish, Louisiana. He is holding a photograph of another of his handmade boats.

97

BIRDHOUSES & FEEDERS

Throughout history, wherever people have depended upon plants and animals for sustenance, the insects and predators who share their culinary preferences have been an annoyance or, at worst, a threat to life. Although in recent years the standard defense against pests has been the widespread use of chemical poisons, the easiest and ecologically safest method of controlling their population is to enlist nature's aid by providing appropriate shelter and food for a variety of birds.

Many elderly residents throughout the South recall the effectiveness of this old method of "companion farming." One Tennessean whose mother raised chickens recalls, "My mother had about 150 hens. We'd sell the chickens and the eggs to get the little things we needed—coal, oil, sugar, and so on. We had a martin house to keep the bee martins around our home here because they would surely whip a hawk or anything.

Feeding stations allow birds easy access to the seeds and nuts placed inside.

Double-decker birdhouses are ideal for small birds.

Some birdhouses reflect the log construction of the maker's own home. The small branch "logs" of the small scale version are notched together in the traditional manner.

No other bird would come around where a bee martin was!"

Success in luring birds depends upon providing them with adequate food and shelter. Although expensive and elaborate birdhouses can be purchased, some of the most attractive can be made from trees and bushes where the birds congregate.

Hollow logs, which are natural nesting places for many species, can easily be made into birdhouses. First, a section is cut off, then the rotted wood on the inside scraped away with a long-handled chisel. Next, a thin slice from a smaller log or a piece of scrap plywood is used to plug the bottom end of the hollow log and form the floor. For the door, a small hole is drilled in the face of the log just big enough for an adult bird to enter; if there is a knot, it can be removed for a natural hole. Finally, the top end of the log is cut off to support a roof shape that is shingled with overlapping slabs of outer bark nailed into place. A protruding twig can be attached in front of the door to provide the bird with a perch.

Feeding birds, necessary only in winter months, should be done in another, more open structure where many birds can congregate at once. Fruits that many species enjoy include small pieces of apples, raisins, fresh coconut, and cranberries. Peanut butter mixed with cornmeal and suet or shortening is a good high-energy fat and protein diet that birds like. Hard-shelled nuts, such as pecans and walnuts, cracked open and placed in the feeder, will be pecked clean. The Audubon Society recommends this "no waste" mixed seed blend: 30 percent shelled sunflower seeds, 15 percent white millet, 15 percent gray millet, 20 percent peanuts, and 20 percent cracked corn. Whatever the choice of food, all ornithologists stress the importance of continuing a feeding program once it is begun, because birds become dependent.

Hollow logs, a natural nesting place for many types of birds, can easily be made into birdhouses by adding a floor, slab roof, and twig perch.

99

SEWING

Many textile traditions, including tatting, have been passed along by Southern women from generation to generation.

Of all the many varieties of textiles handcrafted throughout the South, quilts, samplers, and other examples of needle crafts are undoubtedly the most treasured of family heirlooms.

Bed coverings, the most common of all the traditional needle crafts, were created by virtually all pioneer women in order to provide warmth for their families. Whenever a patterned quilt top was finished and ready to be sewn to its backing, it was the custom in the early settlement days to hold a quilting bee, to which the hostess who "pieced" the top invited as many women as would fit around her quilting frame. As much a social occasion as a work session, the quilting bee gave women the chance to exchange family news, quilt patterns, and fabric scraps as they stitched together the top, stuffing, and backing of the hostess's quilt. The early quilts were a salvage craft that made use of still usable scraps of fabric from worn-out clothing. The bed coverings were then used until they themselves were worn out.

When factory-made bed coverings became available in the mid-1800s, the art of quilting was not replaced and forgotten, as were so many other early craft forms. Instead, quilting became more elaborate and decorative, providing an outlet for creative expression. Countless hours of loving labor turned scraps of fabric into extraordinary works of art. The raw materials of a patchwork quilt, however, were not mere pieces of cloth, but remnants of a family's history. When pieces of a young girl's first communion dress or a boy's first pair of long pants, or "courtin' suit," were stitched together, the resulting quilt could elicit numerous and distinct memories. As family mementos, quilts frequently have been lovingly preserved for generations, right up to the present.

The women settlers of the early South did not limit themselves to the creation of utilitarian quilts and other bed coverings. Many of them filled the hours not spent on other domestic chores by engaging in "fancy work," producing embroidered samplers, exquisite laces, and yards of tatted edging that could be then sewn to their linens. These more decorative needle crafts of embroidery, tatting, and drawnwork (also known as pulled thread work) allowed the women creative expression while providing decorative items to beautify their homes. The traditions of these needle crafts were very widespread, cutting across both class and color barriers. From the humblest cabins to the most elaborate mansions throughout the South, women created the fancy work that enhanced their homes.

For many girls, learning the needle crafts from a mother, an aunt, or a grandmother—who had learned the patterns and traditions from their female forebears—was an essential and important part of their ascension to womanhood and preparation for marriage. In later years, needle crafts provided women with marketable skills. In the Mexican-American communities in Texas, for example, there has long been a tradition of drawnwork and embroidery done for pay. In other communities, nimble quilters have provided their families with extra income by quilting tops hand pieced by others or machine stitched in factories.

Today more people practice needle crafts than any other craft form in the South. Among them are women who continue as their families have for generations, piecing and working patterns that have become as familiar to them as the images in their family photo albums. Whether their reasons for investing countless hours in these traditional needle crafts is purely utilitarian, artistic, or a combination of both, they are maintaining their connections with the past in remarkable and beautiful ways.

QUILTS

Few objects in our history have been so admired and treasured as the quilt. As diverse as the people who create them, quilts have been made in this country since the earliest days of settlement. The origin of quiltmaking, however, goes back much further than the settlement of this country.

Quilting began in America essentially to provide coverings for the family beds, but the technique can be traced back to 3000 B.C. in the quilted clothing of the Middle East and India. It is popularly believed that the craft was brought to Europe by the Crusaders as they returned from their journeys to the East in the twelfth century. During several years of severely cold winters in the fourteenth century, European women adopted quilting techniques to add to the warmth of their bed coverings. From that strictly utilitarian craft evolved one of elaborate decoration.

Although documentation of the work by American colonists is limited, it is believed that the earliest quilts in this country were hurriedly put together, with little or no decoration, to fend off the cold of wilderness winters. Often as many as a half-dozen quilts were piled on each bed in the poorly insulated houses. With an average of ten family members in each household, the women were kept busy constructing summer and winter utility quilts and stuffing them with straw, twigs, or even corncobs.

As soon as families became more settled and their shelter improved, however, quiltmaking became more elaborate. Pioneer women attempted to beautify their homes as well as provide warmth for their families. While quilts continued to be made primarily from scraps of the family's used clothing, the salvage nature of the craft was eventually replaced by more aesthetic interests. Patches were cut more evenly. Colors were combined in pleasing, rather than random, ways. Symmetrical designs and patterns began to emerge. Before long, quiltmaking became the most practiced craft form in America.

The patterns these early quiltmakers developed were clear reflections of their lives and stand as historic documents to their times. Births, deaths, struggles, and joys are all reflected in designs that have been passed down, relatively unchanged, for generations. Some of the patterns, such as Straight Furrow, Barn Raising, and Wagon Wheel, were named for the obvious elements in their daily lives. Others were modeled after things in nature, such as Harvest Sun, North Carolina Lily, and Flying Geese. Still other patterns incorporated religious motifs, such as Star of Bethlehem, Tree of Life, and Forbidden Fruit.

Patterns were freely exchanged from household to household at quilting bees, barn raisings, agricultural fairs, and other gatherings. They were also spread in rural areas by traveling ministers carrying quilt patterns in their saddlebags and by peddlers who, along with pans, knives, and sewing notions, brought news of the latest designs. Pattern pieces were also enclosed in letters that sometimes took weeks, if not months, to travel from one writer to another.

When quilts became worn, their usefulness did not end. They were draped over the inside of doorways to block the cold, used as padding on tractor seats or in the doghouse, and spread over potatoes, apples, or other fruits and vegetables that could not be allowed to freeze; they even became the stuffing for yet another quilt. Another use, common in the South, was as a cover for harvested tobacco plants in the tobacco barn to prevent the leaves from drying out and falling off the stems.

The advent of the twentieth century brought inexpensive, factory-made blankets, insulated houses, and easy access to manufactured textiles. Although the necessity of quilting lessened for most women, the craft has endured. Some still make quilts to keep their families warm, but many others continue their families' quilting traditions despite the central heating that now warms their homes.

Two such women, Louise Barr and her mother, Annie Linder Sheroan, have produced hundreds of quilts over the years, many of them award winners, and are never without a quilt in the quilting frame. There was a strong tradition of quilting in Mrs. Sheroan's family, and she began piecing and quilting as a young girl in her rural Kentucky home in the tradition of her mother and grandmother. She distinctly remembers the patterns and techniques that she learned decades ago.

One design in particular is now in its fourth generation in her family. "My great-aunt lived in a log house," she recalls. "They used corded beds [rope stretched across a bed frame] in those days and laid

Afro-American quilts command attention with their powerful and colorful designs. Mississippi quilter Sarah Mary Taylor followed the traditions of her ancestors, often incorporating strips of cloth as dividers between blocks.

Afro-American quilters often use small, geometric pieces for their quilt tops.

Many eschew the ordered symmetry of Anglo-derived patterns.

They prefer a less formal design, often using unexpected color combinations.

their straw ticks [mattresses] right on the cords. Her bed had this particular quilt on it with a design that looked like it was a cactus, and on the top was a red bird. My mother made a quilt with this same pattern on it, but without the red bird. We used it until it wore out, and then she threw it down into the gully. When she did that, I said, 'Oh, Mama, I wished you had saved that so we could have gotten the pattern.' So she went and got it, and we took the pattern right off and started another quilt!"

She never finished that quilt, but her daughter, Mrs. Barr, has the pieces and plans to use them in a quilt for her own daughters. Mrs. Barr has continued the tradition by making her own quilt based on the pattern, reinstating the red bird from the original design. "I made the top, but Mama quilted it. I wanted her to because it's in the family, and I wanted to know that she was the one who stitched it."

Mrs. Sheroan remembers her mother making calico quilts for summer use, and "overalls" quilts, using worn-out overalls, for winter use, backed with "out-

(Left) Afro-American quilts are often referred to as the visual equivalent of jazz because of their seemingly random and improvisational patterning.

ing," or flannel. They colored many of their fabrics with natural dyes, boiling the cloth with plant materials to obtain different hues—white oak bark for purple, walnut for brown, and hickory for yellow. Their early quilts were often stuffed with wool gleaned from a neighbor's sheep. "They'd call Mama when one of their sheep died, and she would pick the wool off of it and would have me pick it clean, you know, pick all the trash out of the wool. It was the sleepiest job I've ever done!"

While her daughter was young, Mrs. Sheroan used her stitching skills to support the family. For almost two decades she quilted tops for a woman who sold quilts in Florida, and prior to that, she and other women in her rural Kentucky community hand-quilted bedspreads for a commercial bedcovering company for many years. "The tops were in solid colors and already stamped off with the pattern, most of them satin and taffeta. On a certain day of the week, a truck would bring the women to pick up their work and then would take them home. That was the biggest day of the week for us, to bring in our work, pick up more, get our money, and do our grocery shopping. We just had a ball." She quilted an average of three tops a week, earning about two dollars for each one she completed. "That was in the thirties, and that money seemed like a lot then."

Growing up amid this strong quilting tradition, Mrs. Barr began as a young girl to piece her own quilts from sewing scraps. Today she and her mother continue to use "leftover" pieces as well as purchased material and often work together on their quilts. Several years ago, when Mrs. Barr was working on her entry in the Kentucky Heritage Quilt Society competition, she quit to help one of her daughters after surgery. Mrs. Sheroan finished quilting the entry, an intricate star pattern that went on to win the blue ribbon. "You can't tell the difference in our quilting," Mrs. Barr says with pride.

Their way of making quilts has changed very little from settlement days, although the patterns they now use may come from one of the many quilting magazines to which they both subscribe, as well as from memories of past quilts. Most of their patterns involve intricate, tedious appliqué work. Each element of a design is cut from a larger piece of fabric and its edges basted under to prevent unraveling. The separate pieces are basted in place on the quilt top and then permanently slipstitched in place. Each of the quilt tops typically contains hundreds of separately appliquéd pieces and may take several months to complete.

Pieced tops must be layered with a filling, or batting, and a backing and stitched together to make a finished quilt. Before the advent of synthetic fibers, cotton was often used in the South as a readily available insulating filler. The seeds were pounded flat or removed during ginning or by hand. The cotton was then "carded," or combed, into "batts," or layers, which were laid between the quilt top and the backing. Although cotton batting is still available today,

most quiltmakers—Mrs. Sheroan and Mrs. Barr included—prefer polyester because of its washability, its availability, and the ease of working with it.

Traditionally, a quilt frame is used to hold the three layers in place, preventing them from shifting during the stitching. A simple construction of four sturdy lengths of wood held together at right angles by clamps, the early frames were often suspended by ropes from hooks in the ceiling and could be raised out of the way when the room was needed for other uses. Mrs. Sheroan and her daughter still use the same large frame that hung from Mrs. Sheroan's farmhouse ceiling during her childhood. "I never knew about anybody quilting any other way." She would still prefer to hang the frame, but the electric heat in her more modern home is ducted through the ceiling. She therefore supports the frame on the backs of four chairs, a more common contemporary practice.

Mrs. Sheroan pins her backing cloth, usually a piece of purchased fabric, to strips of heavy fabric that are permanently bound to the eges of her frame; then she lays her batting on top of the backing cloth, and her appliquéd top on the batting. After pinning everything together, she winds up the three layers on one of the lengths of the frame, leaving a section exposed for stitching. As she progresses with the quilting, she releases the clamps and lets out more of the fabric sandwich, while winding up the finished portions at the opposite end of the frame.

The quilting of the top to the backing through the layer of stuffing not only holds the batting permanently in place but also functions as an aesthetic element of the finished quilt. Intricate patterns of fine, even stitches have always been one of the most admired characteristics of the European-derived quilting tradition. To assure evenness in the overall stitching pattern, almost all tops are marked in some way before

Making a Patchwork Quilt, *ca. 1930, by Doris Ulmann*.

they are quilted. In early days, templates of heavy paper or tin were used with water-soluble ink to mark the pattern. Mrs. Sheroan marks her pattern on tracing paper, then uses a needle to puncture the design in the paper. She lays the paper on her quilt top and dusts cinnamon over it, rubbing it with a chalkboard eraser to ensure that the spice has penetrated the holes. With the scent of the cinnamon permeating the room, she sits hour after hour, often in tandem with her daughter, taking tiny stitches with a small needle, exactly as her ancestors did to create useful yet magnificent textiles.

Quilts are also familiar objects in black history. A rich heritage of handcrafts, textile skills among them, accompanied the slaves who were brought to this country from areas that are now Senegal, Ghana, Nigeria, Angola, and other parts of Africa where people practiced a wide range of handcrafts. Quiltmaking was an active part of slave life on the plantation. Although the techniques of quilting were largely European in origin, the black women incorporated African-derived design elements into their own quilts, and the result was a distinctly Afro-American patterning tradition that continues to this day.

Like their Anglo-American counterparts, Afro-American quilts are made from pieced or appliquéd tops sewn to a backing with an inner layer of batting, but that is where the similarity ends. Whereas Anglo-American quilts are characterized by a tight, symmetrical design, even and repetitive patterns, and fine, delicate stitching, Afro-American quilts, in contrast, are often characterized by random and asymmetrical patterning, bright colors, and a sense of improvisation that can be compared to jazz.

Among the most common design motifs used by black quilters in the South is strip patterning. Commonly believed to be derived from centuries-old weaving techniques in West Africa—where narrow looms produce strips of fabric whose edges are then sewn together to form larger pieces of cloth—strip patterning appears in Afro-American quilts from Maryland to Texas. Pieces of brightly colored fabric of varying lengths and widths are sewn together into strips, or "strings," which then form patterns on the quilt top and further define spaces. The strips usually do not line up evenly from row to row, and the result is an offset design.

The uniform color schemes seen in most Anglo-American quilts are not typical of Afro-American quilts. Instead, bright colors are used unpredictably,

and they tend to emphasize large designs that can be seen quite easily from a distance in bright sunlight, a throwback to one of the necessary functions of African clothing. Birds, fish, pigs, human forms, and other figurative motifs often appear as appliquéd designs, remnants of the strong communicative function of African textiles.

Multiple patterning—the inclusion of several different patterns randomly arranged on a single quilt top—is also characteristic of Afro-American quilts. Whether derived from the ancient African textile

Log cabin quilts, such as the Streak of Lightening pattern, are created by arranging jagged horizontal bands of color in a herringbone design. Popular throughout the South for generations, this kind of quilt makes striking use of small fabric scraps.

Mrs. Sheroan dusts cinnamon over her pierced paper pattern to transfer the design to her quilt top before stitching.

tradition in which the number of complex patterns on a garment increased with the owner's status, or from the African belief that a jumbled pattern could keep evil spirits at bay, multiple patterning is still used, along with other design forms distinctly African in origin, even though the original meanings have been lost through the generations.

Throughout the South today, the tradition of quiltmaking continues. The basic process of joining two pieces of material with a filling and stitching the three layers together is repeated daily in both rural and urban communities by quiltmakers who combine their sewing skills with their own design traditions. Patterns may be passed down through families, found in quilting journals and books, or improvised. Quilt tops may be pieced with remnants of treasured articles of clothing, carefully chosen purchased fabrics, or scraps from old sewing projects. The finished quilts might be used to keep a child warm, hung on a wall, or put away in a trunk as a family heirloom. Each, however, is a unique record of its creator's life, preserving cultural memories for generations to come.

Mrs. Barr and Mrs. Sheroan reminisce over Mrs. Barr's first quilt pieces, intended for a Double Wedding Ring quilt, saved from her childhood.

She often works in tandem with her daughter, Louise Barr, who is also an avid quilter. Together they delicately stitch Mrs. Sheroan's prizewinning President's Wreath quilt. The frame, which is supported on four chairs, is the same one that hung from Mrs. Sheroan's farmhouse ceiling during her childhood.

Each appliquéd piece on their quilts is hand stitched three separate times before being sewn permanently in place.

EMBROIDERY

Memories of her life in pre-World War II Mississippi are lovingly documented with embroidery by Ethel Wright Mohammad. This piece, called The Storm, *shows most of her children huddling with Mittie, the housekeeper, during a tornado.*

Embroidery, another sewing skill typically passed down from mother to daughter, was considered an essential part of each young woman's repertory of basic sewing techniques. Although the embroidered sampler—actually a catalog of sewing stitches that its maker would use for reference—is no longer a required assignment for every young needleworker, embroidery is still a popular pastime for many.

Ethel Wright Mohammed, like all young girls in the early 1900s in Webster County, Mississippi, learned the craft from her mother. "The ladies in the house would always embroider," she recalls. "My mama made me a little picture book out of cloth and would tell me to go draw. If I'd say, 'I don't know what to embroider,' she'd say, 'Now, I don't have time to draw anything for

Mrs. Mohammad's childhood memories of harp singing at her local church are recorded in cotton and wool on linen.

In The Cotton Pickers, *two young pickers are unaware of the sting worm behind them on the fence, an insect Mrs. Mohammad believed as a child would count your teeth and then cause your death.*

you, so you draw the little cat you love so well.' I would draw him, and then outline him. I knew how to do the little chainstitch, and so I would chainstitch all around him."

Today, using the same skills learned more than seventy years ago, she creates important visual documents of life in the South. Recalling memories of her childhood and her early days as a mother with seven children, she sketches her recollections on linen, outlines them with her chainstitch, and then lovingly fills in each person, animal, and tree with the basic stitches from her childhood. "I like to embroider something from memory," she explains, "something that I lived through, an experience. So I get it in my mind, and I draw my picture out. I get right down with it and I say, 'Now, let's see, this was here, and this must have been there,' you know. As near the facts as can possibly be."

From the two little boys picking cotton, unaware of the "sting worm" crawling on the fence behind them, to her own portrait with her small children and maid during a tornado, she documents, in traditional stitchery, an inspired vision of a South that is now gone forever.

TATTING

Tatting, the craft of making lace by looping and knotting thread, developed during the early 1800s in England and other parts of Europe. It is believed to have originated with the ancient maritime techniques of simple knotting. Its earliest forms were simply strings of knots sewn onto fabric to form a decorative design. Tatting was introduced to America from Europe prior to the Civil War, and the craft remained very popular here through the turn of the century, flourishing in the early 1920s with the regular publication of patterns and instruction booklets, which could be purchased in any local five-and-dime store.

Often dubbed "poor man's lace" because of the common practice of using simple cotton cording to form designs mimicking intricate bobbin laces, tatting is a much easier craft to master than lacemaking. It also produces a much stronger lace, suitable for everyday items on which the use of more delicate laces would be inappropriate.

Tatted lace is made from a series of simple double half-hitch knots, called double stitches, tied over a core thread to make a chain. A length of chain is looped into rings of various sizes which, in turn, are combined to make patterns. A second kind of loop, a picot, is formed by pulling a length of core thread out of its run of double stitches, thereby adding variety to the texture of the basic chain. Unlike bobbin lacemaking, which employs dozens of bobbins to hold apart and weave separate threads, tatting requires only two small shuttles, one containing the spool of core thread, and another the spool from which the double stitches are tied.

Although the basic skills in tatting are relatively easy to learn, the few Southern women who maintain the tradition are finding it difficult to pass on. The current lack of printed literature and patterns for this needle craft means that the skills must be passed on directly from experienced tatter to novice, and the number of people who are willing to spend the long hours required to produce yards of the delicate lacework is dwindling.

Tatting has often been called "poor man's lace" because it uses an easy technique and plain cotton cording to mimic intricate lace patterns.

Unlike more complex lace-making methods, tatted lace is traditionally made from a series of simply made double half-hitch knots.

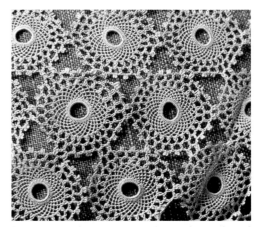

The rings and chains made by the knotted cord are then combined to form patterns, producing a strong lace suitable for everyday use.

114

DRAWNWORK

Drawnwork, also known as drawn thread work and pulled thread work, is one of the earliest known forms of embroidery and can be traced back to the twelfth century. It was introduced to the South by early immigrants from Latin America, where needle crafts were taught as part of every young woman's education. Used to embellish ecclesiastical garments and clothing for special occasions such as weddings and christenings, and for fine linens, this craft tradition continues today, primarily in the Mexican-American communities of Texas.

In drawnwork (*deshilado* in Spanish, meaning "to de-thread"), sections of warp or weft threads are actually pulled from the fabric, leaving a band of parallel threads. These threads are then counted and tied together in small clusters and sometimes used as a foundation for further embroidery, creating patterns that are often as intricate as lace.

Texas needleworker Innocencia Ancira creates drawnwork, also called pulled thread work, by pulling some threads from a piece of fabric and leaving others, providing an open foundation for further embroidery.

MARDI GRAS INDIAN COSTUMES

Of the many craft forms that are associated with festivals throughout the South, costumes and masquerade paraphernalia are among the most dazzling, providing an extraordinary display of the needleworker's art. One of the most highly developed and exquisitely ornate is the masking tradition of the Mardi Gras "Indians" of New Orleans.

Dating from the mid-1800s, the tradition is believed to have originated in the deep South before the Civil War among descendants of escaped slaves who were harbored by various Indian tribes. Today the distinctions between the African and the Indian components of these Mardi Gras celebrations are ill-defined as the cultures have blended. The participants still relate strongly to both cultures, however, with the American Indian tradition most evident in the costuming and the African clearest in the music and dancing.

Although not nearly as well-known as the floats and parades of the Caucasian celebrants, the costumes and foot processions of these black brotherhoods are especially captivating. Each participant makes his own costume, which represents an almost inconceivable personal investment of money, time, and labor.

Prior to World War II, the costuming traditions were not nearly so elaborate as they are today. Ferdinand Bigard, chief of the "tribe" known as the Cheyennes, remembers processions from his childhood. "Before the war, the old Indians wore what I would call a scavenger suit. You know the crates that eggs come in? Well, they would take those, glitter them, and put them on their suits. Then they would go to the can companies and dice little pieces of metal and put them on with ribbon. When the sun hit, they would really shine. The suits were very, very meager back then."

Today the members of more than two dozen tribes spend an entire year constructing the separate pieces of their "outfits," and then they laboriously hand sew

(Right) *Chief Charles Taylor of the White Cloud Hunters wears an elaborate costume that consists of more than a dozen separately made pieces.*

A costume "patch" begins with a freehand pencil sketch on canvas, often an Indian design.

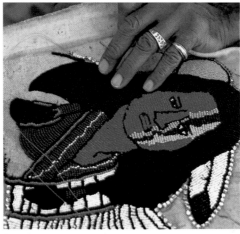

Beads, sequins, feathers, and other decorations are sewn by hand onto the patch.

The heavily embellished patches are then sewn onto the individual foundation garments.

A detail from a costume reveals the mixed heritage of the Mardi Gras Indian groups.

thousands of sequins, beads, rhinestones, ribbons, and feathers to each piece, creating extraordinary garments that are reminiscent of elaborate American Indian war costumes. The basic outfit consists of a vest, an apron, cuffs, leggings, moccasins, and a headdress, and many tribal members add other pieces such as capes and bustles, bringing the weight of their costumes up to as much as 150 pounds, a burden reflected in a song by the late George Landry of the Wild Tchoupitoulas tribe: "Big Chief got a golden crown, golden crown make it drag the ground."

Each piece begins as a piece of canvas, called a "patch," on which a freehand design, usually an Indian motif, is sketched. Each patch is heavily beaded, leaving no canvas to show through, and then, with other patches, is sewn to a larger velvet or satin foundation piece to complete the outfit. The cost of a single outfit often exceeds several thousand dollars, an especially staggering figure when you consider that the

outfit is used for only one year and is worn on only three days during that year—on Mardi Gras day when the tribal processions snake through their separate neighborhoods; during the evening of St. Joseph's Day when the costumes are judged by a jury of retired chiefs and other dignitaries; and on "Super Sunday," the Sunday following St. Joseph's Day, when all of the tribes gather for one big parade. Because of the high cost of the materials, most costumes are dismantled and the parts recycled for the next year's outfits.

Designs for many of the members' costumes are sometimes drawn by the most skilled artists in the group. The techniques of beading and sewing are passed down from the older members of each tribe to the younger ones during sewing parties, where pieces of the costumes are beaded and embellished. The rivalry is so strong, however, even among members of the same tribe, that completed outfits are not unveiled until the day of Mardi Gras.

SCREEN MASK

Another Mardi Gras tradition, practiced only in the eight parishes in southwest Louisiana that are considered Cajun territory, is the *Courir de Mardi Gras*, or "Mardi Gras Run." Starting at daybreak on the festival day, groups of up to one hundred horsemen ride from farm to farm, entering the property at full gallop and then dancing and performing for the farmers. In return for their entertainment, they collect from each farm an ingredient for their communal gumbo, which is served at the end of the day.

The celebrants take great care to conceal their identities. They frequently exchange horses throughout the day so that a rider cannot be recognized by his mount; they disguise their voices by speaking in high falsetto; and they wear costumes, which include gloves to disguise their hands and bizarre masks made of window screening that is painted and shaped to fit the face. With their anonymity thus preserved even among themselves, they can suspend all inhibitions for the day.

In St. Landry Parish, Louisiana, Georgie and Allen Manuel continue the screen mask tradition, making masks for many of the town's residents, some of whom are participants in the local *Courir de Mardi Gras*. They use only metal window screening because plastic window screening will not hold its shape. Mr. Manuel first cuts an eight- to ten-inch square from a large roll of metal screening, then cuts a three-inch slit in the bottom of the piece where the chin will be formed. Using a ball peen hammer, he carefully pounds the screening into the contours of a mold that he made from a two-by-twelve inch piece of pine. Eyes, nose, and chin emerge in three dimensions. Mrs. Manuel hot glues the pieces of the now rounded chin together and glues fabric over the edges so the wearer will not be scratched. After refining the impressions, she paints facial features on the mask. It is then ready to hide the wearer's identity while allowing his facial expressions to show through the screen, grotesquely animating the handiwork.

Screen hammered into a wooden form.

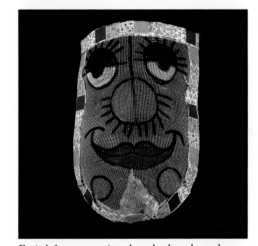

Facial features painted and edges bound.

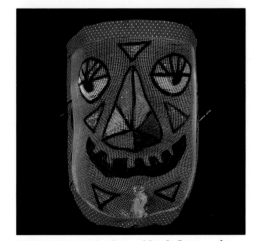

Masks are worn by Cajun Mardi Gras revelers.

WOODCARVING

The decoy, developed hundreds of years ago to lure waterfowl into shooting range, has become one of the most recognizable and popular forms of American folk art.

During the earliest days of settlement, wood was abundant and cheap, making it the primary resource for building. Woodworking and woodcarving skills were therefore as essential to the pioneers as their knowledge of farming and hunting. With a few exceptions, nearly every part of their environment—from the log house to the butter mold in the kitchen—was either built or carved from wood.

By the late 1800s, however, the farm woodlot began to disappear as endless miles of forests were "coaled off," or harvested for the production of charcoal. Charcoal not only fueled the country's growing iron factories, but also was used for hundreds of other purposes, including water purification, the production of printing ink, and even the surfacing of roadbeds. From the factories whose machines were stoked with the precious charcoal came the mass-produced products that gradually replaced most handmade wooden items.

The interest in carving, however, did not

diminish. As happened with the craft of quilt-making, the availability of more and more factory-made products allowed carvers to spend less time producing essentials and more time creating the elaborate, the decorative, and the fanciful. Woodcarving provided men with a means of creative expression, just as patchwork and appliqué did for women.

The tradition continues strongly today. Throughout the South, from the decoy carvers along the Susquehanna Flats of Maryland, to the Houma Indians on the southernmost tip of Louisiana, an astonishing variety of objects both practical and decorative are being whittled, shaved, and carved from what continues to be the most accessible and renewable resource, our native woods.

Each type of wood possesses its own unique set of characteristics, qualities completely familiar to all dedicated carvers. With few exceptions, hardwoods—broad-leafed trees such as wild cherry, walnut, oak, birch, maple, and holly—are heavier than softwoods, more firmly textured, and less likely to warp and shrink. For these reasons and because they take polish and finishing oils well, hardwoods are usually preferred for small carvings. Soft and medium woods—evergreens such as white pine, cedar, and Douglas fir, and also buckeye and butter-nut—are generally used for less exacting larger pieces because they are more easily carved and shaved.

The woodcarver must consider several characteristics of the wood before beginning a piece: the grain (the direction of the fibers), the texture (patterns caused by the growth rings and the structure of the pores), and the figure (a combination of many elements, including form, shape, color, and even the way the wood was sawed). A Maryland decoy carver, for example, will use white pine for the body of a duck because it is so resistant to water damage, but might choose basswood for the head because, as a softer wood, it is easier to work by hand. Tool-handle carvers throughout the South will choose hickory for its strength, density, and straight grain, which allows the "pole" of wood to split evenly. And Cherokee carvers will often create breathtaking sculptures from walnut and wild cherry, making the grain of the wood an integral part of the design.

In a partnership as graceful, sensitive, and enduring as dance, Southern carvers have continued through the generations to select and sculpt their native woods, revealing in ways both practical and expressive the warmth, fragrance, and unlimited bounty of this varied and wonderfully rich resource.

DECOYS & DECORATIVE BIRDS

Long before the first Englishman set foot on the shore where the Chesapeake Bay meets the Susquehanna River in Maryland in the early 1600s, the area, known as the Susquehanna Flats, had become one of the largest estuaries and waterfowl feeding grounds on the continent. Before dams were built and the flow of the river halted, eel grass and wild celery grew in such abundance that each autumn birds by the hundreds of thousands stopped to feed during their journey from breeding grounds in the North to their Southern winter homes.

The early Paiute Indians who lived along the banks of the Susquehanna Flats often used decoys and artificial birds, as well as actual dead ducks, to lure the migrating ducks, geese, and other fowl within killing range. Rushes and reeds were bent and woven into duck shapes and colored with natural pigments or adorned with real duck feathers.

The early English and European settlers who arrived in the late 1600s and early 1700s improved on the Indian designs, replacing the reeds and rushes with more durable, and realistically painted, wood. Many accounts of duck hunting with wooden decoys, some of which predate the American Revolution, were published in England by men who had visited the colonies and participated in duck-hunting forays.

By the middle of the nineteenth century, the country's appetite for the succulent waterfowl spawned a new breed of gunner: the market hunter. Prompted by fine restaurants along the Eastern seaboard willing to pay as much as five dollars for a good pair of "cans," or canvasback ducks, these hunters devised incredible methods to bring down the ducks by the thousands. They gunned at night using lights and dozens of shot-guns. Some used small cannons that fired up to a pound of shot at once. The most destructive method of all, however, was the use of the sinkbox.

Essentially a large rectangular or coffin-shaped wooden box with broad flaps hinged on all four sides, the sinkbox was floated out on the water with its flaps opened out. Enough heavy cast-iron decoys were placed on the wide flaps to keep the sinkbox at water level, and as many as five hundred additional wooden decoys were deployed. The hunter lay waiting in the box until the decoys attracted the ducks, then blasted his shotgun into the flock, killing scores of birds.

The increasing demand for decoys, not only from market hunters, but also from sports hunters and duck clubs, which were common by the late 1800s, spurred many of the men who had been chopping out decoys for themselves to begin making them for sale to others. Because the demand was too great for the handcarvers to accommodate, decoy factories sprang up to supply the market-hunting industry with cheap, wooden ducks. As the hunting season approached, advertisements for these factory-made products would begin to appear in magazines and newspapers. "It's Duck Season, boys," read one ad. "Time to get out the old gun, the boots and—say—how about your decoys? It takes more than luck to stop that flying squadron. It takes a decoy that looks so much like a real live bird that it will fool the wise old duck that rides the wind at the head of the 'V.' Mason's decoys are perfect in shape and coloration. Send today for interesting booklet."

These wholesale hunting methods proved to be all too effective. The wildfowl population that had seemed limitless was quickly reduced. Some species were depleted almost to the point of extinction while

1. *After roughly shaping the duck's body with a band saw, Mr. Vincenti clamps it into a duplicating lathe alongside a full-sized body pattern and duplicates the body in the raw wood.*

2. *He turns as many as several hundred bodies on the lathe before going on to the next steps.*

3. *Even though much of the initial shaping of today's decoys is done with electric saws and lathes, the refining and finish carving are still done by hand with spokeshaves and drawknives.*

4. *Using a drawknife, Mr. Vincenti slices off the place on the neck where the head will be attached after it, too, is carved.*

5. *He sands the neck smooth and then sets the body aside to await the head.*

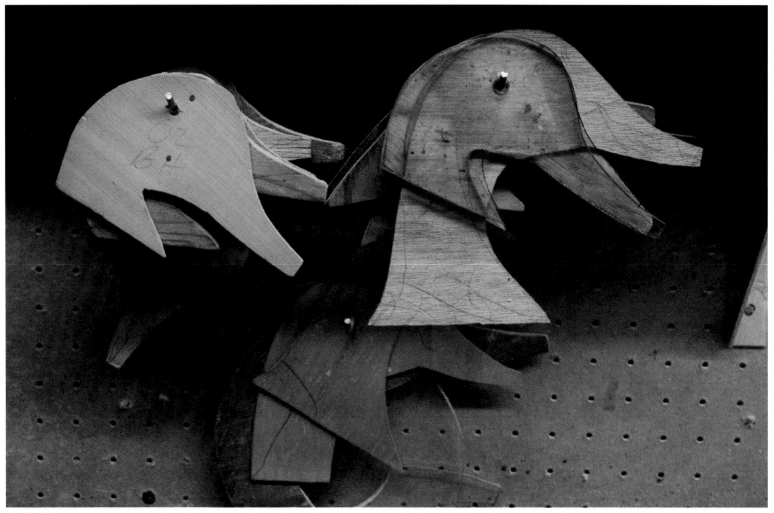

6. *Mr. Vincenti uses a variety of cardboard, wooden, and acrylic patterns to cut the heads for his decoys, some of them his own design and some handed down from the older carvers in his community.*

others were wiped out completely. Recognizing the danger to the wildfowl species, Congress passed a series of Migratory Bird Acts between 1913 and 1918, severely curtailing hunting during the spring breeding period, banning night shooting with lights, and, most importantly, making illegal the sale of all waterfowl. In a final attempt to ban the wholesale slaughter of these birds, the use of sinkboxes was outlawed in 1934.

The elimination of market hunting sharply reduced the need for decoys, and the factories went out of business. The core of handcarvers, however, con-tinued their production, which they had maintained despite the intrusion of the factory-made products. Among them was R. Madison Mitchell, a lifelong resident of Havre de Grace, Maryland, on the edge of the Susquehanna Flats, and the son of a farmer who had gunned and fished to supplement his income.

Mr. Mitchell first began making decoys in 1924 at the age of twenty-three when his cousin, Sam Barnes, asked for his help in completing some orders. According to Mr. Mitchell, when he agreed to help, his cousin had asked him, "What do you know about

7. After the initial shape of the head is rough cut with the band saw, he locks it into his "backyard made" head vise for further handwork.

8. Finally, after dozens of separate steps, the head is attached to the body of the decoy with nails and glue, the holes and cracks are filled in with wood putty, and the entire duck is sanded once again in preparation for priming and painting.

making decoys?" Mr. Mitchell had replied, "The same as you did when you got started." "We'll try it," Mr. Barnes said.

Using nothing but a hatchet to chop out the rough bodies from white pine, then refining them with draw-knives and spokeshaves, Mr. Mitchell soon began turning out canvasbacks, redheads, and blackheads, selling each for little more than a dollar. Two years later Sam Barnes died of pneumonia, and Madison Mitchell took over the decoy business, which he added to his occupation as the town's undertaker.

In the years following his cousin's death, Mr. Mitchell began to refine the design of his decoys. He put a higher roll on the tops of the bodies. He increased the taper of the tails and made the heads more rounded and less angular so that the decoys became more realistic. He also improved the ballast, weighting the ducks more carefully, which resulted in better performance. Decoys made by Madison Mitchell quickly became known as the best in the region, largely due to his attention to detail.

Duane Henry, owner of the Susquehanna Trading

Five examples of canvasback ducks show the different painting styles of their Maryland creators.

Company in Havre de Grace and a local historian, recalls a story typifying Mr. Mitchell's perfectionism. "The carvers always did their woodwork during the summertime, but they wouldn't do any painting during the hot, humid weather because the paint wouldn't dry. In the fall, right before the gunning season, they would paint their birds to sell at hunting time. Back in the winter of 1932, during the Depression, it came time for hunting season. Mr. Mitchell wanted three and a half dollars each for his decoys, but nobody had any money. Fellows would come to him and offer seventy-five cents or a dollar for them, and he decided he wasn't going to sell them. So he kept all his decoys that winter and didn't sell a one. Instead, he spent the winter, when he'd usually be working, having the men who killed birds on the Flats bring them in for study. He measured them, traced them, and remade all of his patterns that winter, as lifelike as possible in size, coloration, and feathering, just to improve his product. Since that winter, he's probably had the most realistic birds that anybody ever made. They are as close to perfection as you can get in a tool."

(Right) *The canvasback drake decoy in front was made by Samuel Barnes in 1920. Behind it is one his student, Madison Mitchell, made in 1954.*

A variety of antique and contemporary gunning decoys made from wood and cork hang on the wall of a Maryland home. Notice the sleeping position of the duck at the upper left.

Although he is now legally blind and no longer carving, Mr. Mitchell's patterns live on, passed down to younger carvers in the area. Pat Vincenti, who as a teenager worked with Mr. Mitchell, is one heir. Unlike most decoymakers who carve in addition to "steady" work, Mr. Vincenti makes decoys full time.

The wood of choice for making decoys along the Chesapeake Bay is white pine, which is prized for its dense grain and resistance to water damage. In order to keep the cost of his ducks down, Mr. Vincenti avoids kiln-dried lumber and buys green wood at one-third the price. Because the wood takes years to dry sufficiently, he buys it four to five years in advance, often tying up thousands of dollars in raw lumber. "The old-timers say it takes a year to dry an inch," he explains. "So if you have a piece of wood that's five inches thick, it takes five years to dry it."

Once the wood is properly seasoned, he makes his initial cut with a table saw. He then clamps the rough shape in a duplicating lathe alongside a full-sized body pattern, either one of Mr. Mitchell's or one of his own design, and duplicates the shape in the new wood.

Working decoys are weighted on the bottom with hand-poured lead ballast to right the bird when it is thrown into the water, as seen on decoys made by R. Madison Mitchell in 1940.

In contrast to their counterparts in Maryland, who use pine and basswood to make decoys, craftsmen in Louisiana most often use light, durable cypress and tupelo gum.

Although most decoy carvers now use electric saws and lathes to shape the bodies, these tools cut only a very crudely shaped form, and a great deal of work must be done by hand. "Even when cut with a duplicating lathe," explains Duane Henry, "they're not finished by any means. It's still about 85 percent handwork. The blank that's turned out by the machine just has the excess removed, which they used to do with a hatchet. One decoymaker told me that he once counted fifty-seven times he handled the decoy from the time he started making it to the time he finished it!"

Using a spokeshave, Mr. Vincenti next shaves the body smooth, further defining the breast and tail of the duck, and then sands the form. Finally, using his drawknife, he cleanly slices off the spot where the head will sit and puts the body aside.

Working from a variety of cardboard, wooden, and even heavy plastic patterns, he cuts the heads from basswood, a lighter wood that is easier to carve than the dense pine. The heads are also rough cut with the band saw, clamped in a "head vise" for further shaping with the drawknife and spokeshave, then whittled with a pocketknife until just right. After sanding the head smooth, Mr. Vincenti attaches it to the waiting body with glue and nails, countersinking the nails and filling in the holes with wood putty.

Although it is an accepted and common practice to use the patterns of the older decoymakers, each carver develops his own painting style. The colors are fairly similar from carver to carver, but the designs and brush techniques are all quite different. "They all have very distinct styles," says Mr. Henry. "We can look at a decoy and tell you who painted it."

After priming the duck with three to four coats of primer, filling nicks in the wood and then sanding between each coat, Mr. Vincenti paints the wing patches first and follows immediately with the final coat of finish paint so that the colors will blend together while still wet. On some ducks such as mallards and black ducks, he will "scratch paint" the final dark coat, scraping through to the lighter base coat with a sharp tool to further define the feather patterns. Only oil-based flat colors are used because a shiny surface will reflect sunlight and scare the ducks away.

(Right) *The diversity of waterfowl in Louisiana, right at the junction of the Mississippi and Central flyways, is reflected in this collection of Louisiana decoys belonging to New Orleans carver Al Muller.*

Most decorative carvers work in stages on many birds at once.

Louisiana decorative carver John Parfait scribes the wing texture onto his birds with an electric burner, using strokes only one quarter inch in length to ensure uniform lines.

With each successive generation, hunters and collectors of these wooden sculptures have demanded more and more detail, even though it is commonly known that ducks will be lured as easily to a crudely shaped and colored decoy as to an elaborately carved bird. The carvers, however, seem unruffled by the demands. "These ducks are more or less painted to meet the gunner's eye, not the duck's eye," explains Mr. Vincenti. "The old-style chunk decoys worked just as good as these ones we spend hours doing. But to meet the gunner's eye, we have to do a good job."

The current interest in realistic carving, coupled with a rapid increase in the collecting mania for antique decoys, has not only allowed the craft to thrive but has also spawned a successful variation: decorative bird carving. Gently derided by carvers of gunning decoys as "circus ducks" because of their brighter, fancier colors and stark realism, they are as highly personal to their carvers as "working" decoys are to their makers. "Endless hours go in to make them as lifelike as possible," says Mr. Henry. "Some of the feathers are even carved separately and inserted into

The cork body Canadian geese decoys in sleeping and feeding positions by Virginia craftsman Jim McInteer have wooden necks, heads, and tail sections, which provide balance in the water.

the bird so that they stand out. It's always a shock when you see a really good one. It looks soft, and when you go to touch it, you don't expect it to be hard."

Across the continent in Louisiana, carver John Parfait, a Houma Indian who has studied and carved birds for a decade, is typical of the decorative woodworkers who might spend hours working on the texture of a single wing. Using a sharpened soldering iron to etch the pattern into the wood, he explains, "If you go real fast, the temperature will diminish and the line will be wider at the bottom. So in order to get the uniform line, you can only take a quarter-inch stroke."

Most decorative birds are painted with acrylic paints rather than the oils used on working decoys. The brighter range of hues and the greater availability of iridescent, metallic colors help the decorative carver simulate the reflection of sunlight off the densely patterned feathers on the backs of the birds.

In decoy carving, as in many other traditional crafts, the line separating the functional from the decorative is impossible to draw clearly. What began as simply a device to draw waterfowl into shooting range has developed into one of the most sought-after and diversely expressed forms of Southern folk craft.

Because geese are both nearsighted and naturally curious, they can be lured with a much simpler decoy like a Maryland "flattie," which is made of Masonite.

TOOL HANDLES

In times past, when timber was cut and shaped locally for an almost unlimited number of uses, ranging from the construction of houses to fuel for cook fires, and when each homestead depended on a garden that was tilled, planted, and weeded by hand, tools such as broad axes, wood mauls, and hoes were common. The metal heads of these tools, most often made by the local blacksmith in those early days, were later widely available through mail-order catalogs and at general stores by the late 1800s. The tool handles, however, were not commercially made. Instead, craftsmen in each community—in many cases the tool owner himself—would fabricate them by splitting hickory logs to the approximate size and then carefully shaving the handles by hand with drawknives.

Today most tool handles are made in small factories situated near substantial stands of ash, which is a more abundant wood than hickory. Large trees are lumbered, brought to the mill by truck, and then ripped apart with circular saws before final shaping on an electric lathe. Despite the apparent saturation of the market by these factory-made products, however, there are still several people in the South who continue to produce tool handles entirely by hand. They work with the traditional hickory, which, they claim, cannot be equaled for strength and durability.

Everett Druien, a Kentucky tool-handle maker who has been working with wood since his youth, is one of those craftsmen who prefers hickory to any other wood. "There's a big difference in timber," he says, "and hickory's hard to beat. It's hard and tough." Although any hickory tree can provide lumber with a strength roughly similar to that of tempered steel, the

Jason Reed, Chairmaker, *ca. 1933, by Doris Ulmann.*

best trees grow in valleys where there is little sun. The trees are forced to reach straight up for the light instead of branching out, and as a result they have fewer knotholes and therefore a straighter grain. Because the grain in young saplings that are five to eight inches in diameter is still tight and less coarse than older trees, they are preferred.

Working with only a hatchet, Mr. Druien splits the "poles," or logs, as soon after cutting as possible, while they are easier to work. He chops them into lengths suitable for handles and hacks off the bark, which can harbor insects if left on the logs. "My uncle told me to cut the timber in the fall after the sap goes out," Mr. Druien recalls, "and remove the bark in November, so

Mr. Richardson begins each handle by roughly shaping it on his homemade lathe.

Although most of today's tool handles are mass produced in factories, there are still men like Kentucky handlemaker Joe Richardson who prefer to produce individual handles to fit each tool.

Kentuckian Everett Druien works his shapes on his shaving horse using a drawknife.

the worms won't get in it. If the bark is left on, worms will hatch out under that bark and eat away back in the wood."

After letting the wood season for several months, Mr. Druien halves and quarters the lengths into "blanks" until the desired diameter for each handle he plans to make is approximated. With a blank of hickory held rigid by a foot-operated clamp, he sits at his shaving horse and patiently shapes the handle with a plane and a drawknife, using the grain of the wood as his guide.

Although some handles are made for stock tools, many are custom carved for particular tools. Repairing or, more exactly, replacing worn or broken handles constitutes a large share of the business. Often the making of a new handle is not the most difficult part of the job. "Some people will leave their handles out in the weather," Mr. Druien says, "and, of course, that's not good for them. Some people bring an ax, the handle broken, and it'll be all swollen up. It's more trouble to get that handle out than it is to replace it! I take a drill, usually, and drill some holes down through the handle and make a little space, then knock it out."

Like most handlemakers, Mr. Druien prefers to carve his handles from hickory because it is a tough and durable wood.

WALKING CANES

Although practiced by whittlers throughout the South, the craft of cane carving has traditionally been the domain of the elderly and the infirm. Many canemakers, after a lifetime of whittling, make their first cane for personal use and, typically, go on making them for others out of pure pleasure.

One such man, Tennessee canemaker Parks Townsend, began to specialize in the craft when an automobile accident left him unable to work. "In just a wink of an eye, it took me out of commission," he explains. "I couldn't do anything on my feet. When I got crippled, well, I didn't want to give up. I just knew I had to figure out something to do. I don't know why I settled for this carvin' and whittlin', but I got to carvin' these canes, and the more I carve, the more I want to!"

Unlike some canemakers who split large logs into dozens of "sticks," Mr. Townsend works with small saplings, using the unique formations of each one to produce a single cane. "I don't split nothin'. I just get them from the size of a wrist on down to real small.

Then I take one and carve it out. I only get one cane out of a stick." Although he is no longer able to gather his own sticks, friends and neighbors keep him supplied with wood. "There's always somebody out looking for me. I never have trouble at all keeping material to work on."

Whether the canemaker's product is meant to be used as an accessory of sartorial splendor or as a simple stick to lean on, hardwoods are always preferred for their toughness and strength. In addition to several varieties of oak, dogwood, and sassafras, Mr. Townsend likes "sourwood" from the sorrel tree, a strong, tightly grained wood with thick bark. "I'll carve just anything that grows up and is shaped like it'll make a good cane, but sourwood makes the best canes. You can hardly ever get it these days, but I believe I'll have to say that sourwood is just about the most durable of anything."

One of his most popular canes, a snake style carved

(Right) *Working with small saplings, Mr. Townsend often uses their unique formations to produce one-of-a-kind canes.*

Tennessee cane carver Parks Townsend claims, "The more I carve, the more I want to!"

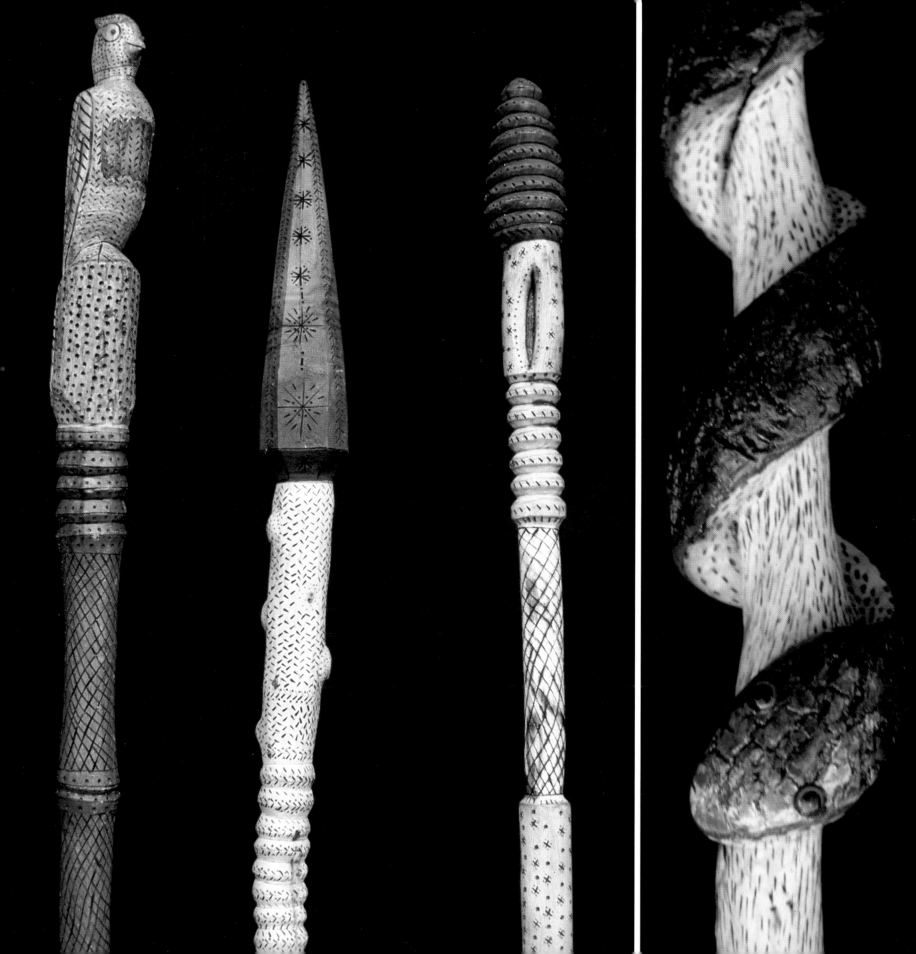

by canemakers throughout the wooded areas of the South, is made from young saplings that have grown within the spiraling grasp of honeysuckle or grapevine. Working with a simple pocketknife, Mr. Townsend follows the natural twist of the stick, whittling the bark from the inner sections and leaving it intact on the outer parts to form the serpent's skin. After carefully shaping the head from the thickest part of the wood, he often sets in beads for the eyes to make the snake more realistic.

Snakes and other reptilian forms, including lizards, turtles, and alligators, in addition to images of the human figure carved in full relief, have also appeared frequently in the work of Afro-American cane carvers. Reminiscent of the conjuring canes tossed into the air by African holy men to capture the attention of the gods, the popular sculptural medium of decorated canes can still be seen in the work of many of the most outstanding Afro-American carvers throughout the South today.

Luster Willis, a Mississippi cane carver, began his work on walking sticks in the early 1930s, vowing to put a cane in the hand of every person in his small community. The simply made canes, unadorned except for the owner's name or a Bible verse incised on the staff, were sold for as little as seventy-five cents each, helping him to survive the hard years of the Depression.

Later, after Mr. Willis observed a man in town whittling on a piece of cedar, his essentially utilitarian canes began to evolve into artistic works. Today most of his canes, which are still hand carved from cedar heartwood, sport full figures at their tops, with arms that are tightly held to the bodies or folded across the chests.

(Left) Snakes, other reptilian forms, and human faces carved in full relief are all popular motifs found on Southern carved canes.

Mississippi carver Luster Willis began making canes in the early 1930s and continues carving today. Most of his canes sport full figures at their tops.

CHAIN CARVING

Whether used to demonstrate knife-handling and carving skills, to meet a challenge, or merely to pass the time, the popular form of whittling known as chain carving has endured throughout the South for generations. The carver begins by outlining a pattern on a long, narrow piece of soft wood, such as linden, soft pine, or cedar. Then, using a simple pocketknife, the carver cuts away the excess from the block of wood.

It's hard to believe that the objects made by chain carving come from one piece of wood. There may be single or double lengths of chain; wooden balls that roll unimpeded through cylindrical or hexagonal cages; and even delightful combinations of both!

Beginning with a single block of wood, whittlers throughout the South pass the time by creating an astounding array of balls trapped in cages.

With only the aid of a pocketknife, the carver releases freely dangling links of chain, creating visual puzzles that confound and delight the viewer.

FOLK SCULPTURE

An exquisite bear sculpture by Amanda Crowe, one of today's leading Cherokee carvers, is made of the rich walnut that grows on her North Carolina reservation.

Although not strictly a Southern tradition, decorative woodcarving has remained a widespread craft in the South and is especially prevalent among the inhabitants of the Appalachian and Great Smoky Mountain ranges where wood is still plentiful.

Among these communities, the Eastern Band of the Cherokee Indians in North Carolina maintains one of the strongest traditions of whittling and sculptural carving in America, as evidenced by the more than seventy registered carvers in their community crafts outlet, the Qualla Arts and Crafts Cooperative in the town of Cherokee, North Carolina. Betty DuPree, manager of the cooperative, explains that the Cherokees have a seemingly innate ability to carve. "They've always done it," she says. "In the early, early days, it was bowls, spoons, and utensils, something to eat with, and toys for the children. Nowadays, they are catering to tourism, carving more to meet the public's interest and demand. But it's something that nobody has ever really learned. They've just always been able to do it."

Many of the older carvers in the community did seem to be born with the ability. In recalling her earliest memories of Amanda Crowe and Goingback Chiltoskey, two of the leading Cherokee carvers, Mrs. DuPree says, "I was in school with Amanda way back before anybody else was carving. She always had a knife. I was scared to death of her! I had to eat at the same lunch table with her and she always had that knife. She was carving with it, but I never knew that. She always had something in her hand, but all I ever saw was the knife. And my mother was in Goingback Chiltoskey's class, and she said *he* carved constantly.

So they just start from the cradle, I guess, with that knife."

Although they have adapted their carving techniques somewhat to changes in technology—band saws have replaced hatchets for making the initial rough cut, and finer grades of sandpaper and oil are used to finish the pieces—the Cherokees still prize the traditional carving woods of buckeye, walnut, and wild cherry for their rich color and smooth grain and especially for their availability on the reservation. "Most everybody has a few trees on their land," explains Mrs. DuPree. "When somebody cuts a tree or if the wind blows one down, by the time it hits the ground, there are people wanting to buy it or claim it."

Today the tradition of passing down the skills from older carver to younger has become more formalized, with many young Cherokees learning the skills in carving classes taught by Amanda Crowe and other master carvers at the local high school. The Cherokee influence has even been felt as far south as Dulac, Louisiana, where some of the leading Cherokee carvers were sent by the federal government's Indian Arts and Crafts Board several years ago to teach the craft to members of other Native American tribes. John Parfait, a Louisiana Houma Indian who has been carving since the age of six, warmly remembers those training sessions with the Cherokees. "I used to carve a bit before, mostly pirogues," he says. "Then when the Cherokees showed up, they opened up a whole new world by sharpening our eyes."

Decorative woodworking is not, however, limited to people who live in forested areas. Although they lack the support of a communal tradition, many carvers and decorative woodworkers can be found working individually in towns and cities throughout the South. Kentuckian Marvin Finn is one such craftsman who, in decades of work, has created an increasingly fanciful

Another bear of walnut was carved by a student in Amanda Crowe's high school class, where she teaches her carving traditions to the next generation.

The Cherokee influence has been felt as far south as Louisiana, as seen in a bear carved by LeMay Walls of St. Mary Parish.

Decorative woodcarving is a strong tradition throughout the South, both in areas where wood is naturally abundant and in more urban regions.

menagerie in his small apartment in a downtown Louisville housing project.

One of thirteen children of poor Alabama farmers, he was raised without the luxury of store-bought toys. Learning knife-handling skills from his father, he began at an early age to whittle and construct his own playthings. Today, working in a cramped kitchen cluttered with wooden sculptures in all stages of completion, he continues to carve and construct flocks of six-foot-tall flamingos, teams of oxen pulling wagons, and scores of intricate, movable toys from assorted pieces of wood he finds in the scrap box of a neighborhood lumber yard.

Unlike the Cherokee carver who prizes the rich and lustrous natural coloration and grain of native hardwoods, Mr. Finn prefers a painted finish on his predominantly plywood pieces. Selecting colors from the random assortment of paints that come his way, largely through donations, Mr. Finn covers his birds and other animals with intensely vivid dashes, dots, and streaks of color, laying them down with apparently inexhaustible spontaneity.

For such woodcarvers as these, whether urban or rural, individual or tribal, there is always an enchanting interplay between the observed reality and their stylized expressions. The necessity that drives them to create, however altered by the passing years, remains rooted in the spirit and the imagination.

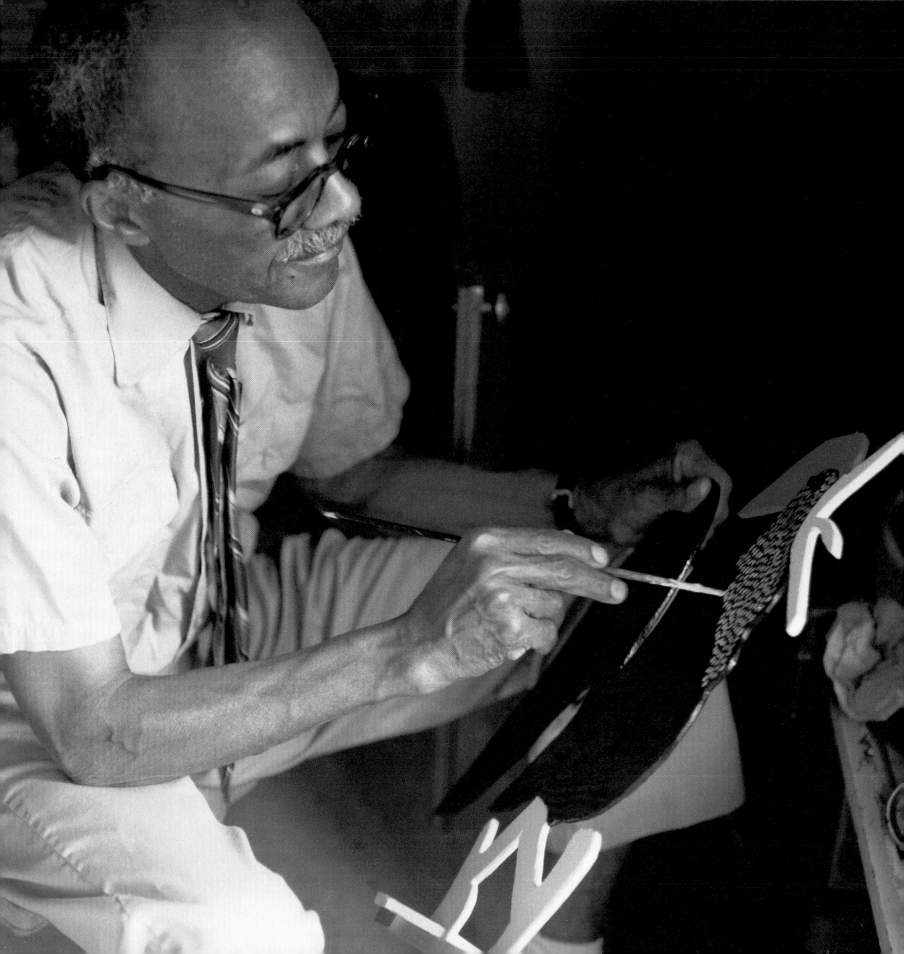

(Left) *Kentuckian Marvin Finn creates a menagerie from scrap wood.* (Above) *With donated paints, he achieves vivid effects.*

Louisiana carver Cyril Billiot also paints his carved birds, but prefers a more realistic interpretation of color.

THE BRASSTOWN CARVERS

I n the early part of this century, residents of mountain communities in North Carolina, like other rural inhabitants throughout the country, faced increasing economic hardship. For complex reasons generated by the national and world economies, they found it more and more difficult to make a living from their farms, and younger generations of would-be farmers were lured away by lucrative factory work in nearby cities.

An educator named John Charles Campbell, who traveled extensively throughout the mountain ranges talking to the people and learning of their needs, became devoted to the idea of a "folk school" that would focus primarily on teaching practical day-to-day skills to rural young adults. Although he died in 1919 without seeing his dream fulfilled, his wife, Olive Dame Campbell, continued his work. In 1925, with the help of her friend Marguerite Butler and with

The wide variety of native woods in forests of the Campbell Folk School provide ample resources for the Brasstown Carvers.

Rooster Carved by a Member of the Brasstown Carvers, ca. 1930.

After the wood is harvested and seasoned, it is cut into roughly shaped "blanks" using patterns as old as the school itself.

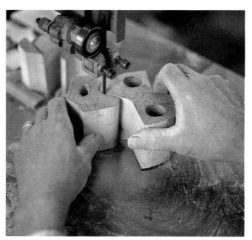

Some wood is then cut with a band saw into blanks for napkin rings.

strong support from the surrounding North Carolina communities, Mrs. Campbell opened the John C. Campbell Folk School in the mountains near Brasstown.

From its inception, the school was dedicated to fostering pride in the rich, cultural heritage of the area's residents while teaching them agricultural and household skills that could help them to support their rural lives. In Miss Butler's words, the idea, controversial in those days of strict, traditional academic standards, was to create a school for the mountain people "where they could learn to farm and keep house, not one that made just teachers and preachers."

Shortly after the school's successful opening, Mrs. Campbell noticed that the men and boys who congregated on the front porch of the local general store spent a good deal of their time whittling as they visited with one another. Acting on her philosophy of encouraging the development of native skills as a means toward economic sustenance, she persuaded them to channel their carving energy into creating specific pieces, drawing their inspiration from the birds and animals familiar to them. It wasn't long before many families were actually earning a better living from carving than they were from farming.

Today, more than fifty years later, the small sign announcing the John C. Campbell Folk School, "All Visitors Welcome," still proclaims the open spirit of the institution, which is nestled comfortably on more than three hundred acres of hardwood forests and flowering meadows in western North Carolina. Throughout the years, the school has adjusted to the adoption of technological advances in agriculture, and today it specializes in teaching traditional crafts and music not only to the residents of nearby mountain communities but to thousands of others who come from all over the world to attend homesteading, craft, and music classes. Despite changes in the school's focus, however, the group that became known as the Brasstown Carvers has continued to produce thousands of exquisite wooden sculptures year after year, becoming one of the most successful cottage industries in the South.

All of the pieces produced by the Brasstown Carvers begin as trees from the school's hardwood forests and other nearby properties. Buckeye, wild cherry, black walnut, butternut, and holly are harvested, then cut into slabs at the school's sawmill and left to season in

After the form is initially shaped on a band saw, a table saw is used to slice rough, angel-shaped ornaments from thick pieces of holly.

The blanks are purchased by the carvers at minimal cost, carved, then resold to the school.

open sheds. Once dry, the slabs are cut with electric saws into roughly shaped "blanks" that are based on flat metal and cardboard patterns as old as the carving group itself.

Each Friday, members of the Brasstown Carvers—including some of the original members from half a century ago, who now carve with their daughters and sons—come to the school from the surrounding hills, carrying baskets filled with their week's work. Kicking mules, howling coon dogs, fluttering geese, blooming dogwood blossoms, lop-eared bunnies are all carved from blanks that carvers have purchased from the school at minimal cost the previous Friday. Each piece is inspected for quality and, if found to meet the standards of the group, is bought back from the carver at a substantially higher rate.

After several coats of finishing oil are applied, the pieces are sold in gift shops at the school and throughout the United States. Finally, to complete the circle and to enable the John C. Campbell Folk School and the Brasstown Carvers to continue their work, the proceeds from the sales of the lovely wooden sculptures come back to the school, supporting both its programs and, through them, the mountain people.

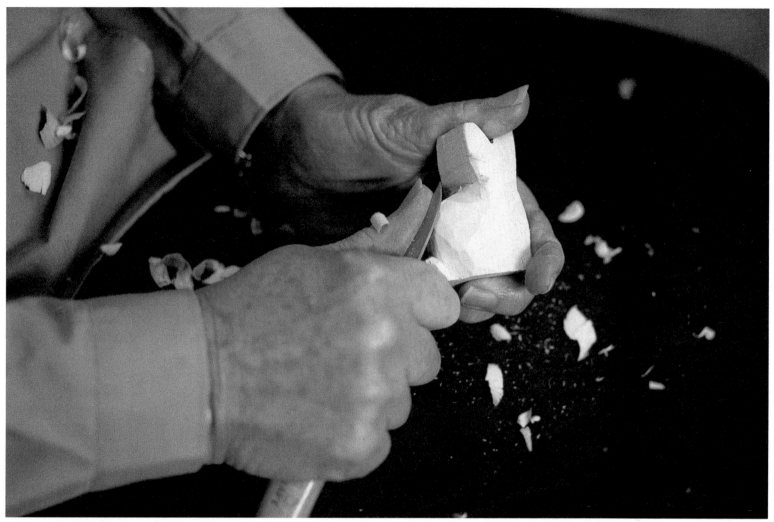

A bunny is carved from a roughly shaped blank.

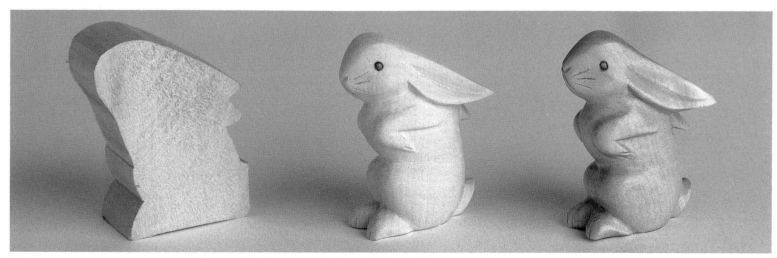

After it is carved, the bunny is finished with oils to bring out the luster of the wood.

153

MASKS

While many Cherokee craft traditions have been irreversibly altered and many others simply lost, some have survived with the configurations—if not necessarily the spirit of the ancient practices—intact. Among them, the custom of maskmaking, although imminently endangered, holds tenuously to its original forms.

One of the most commonly recognized types of mask among Native Americans is the wooden decoy, carved in the likenesses of bears, buffalo, and other wildlife. In the past, hunters wore these masks during ceremonial dances to ensure a bountiful catch and then during the hunt in order to approach the animal without suspicion. Another mask form created by the Cherokees was the sacred rattlesnake mask, a human face with a rattlesnake curled on top of the head, used only by the medicine man to facilitate curing and by the warrior to announce his intention to do battle.

(Left) Cherokee carver Will Long sits outside his mountainside home and begins to shape a rattlesnake mask from a just-halved buckeye log.

The mask most frequently produced by the Cherokees, at least in the years following the arrival of white settlers, was the Booger mask, carved to represent "people far away or across the water"—the Europeans, blacks, and other Indian tribes—who brought with them sickness, pollution, and death. As legend goes, a spirit named Stone Coat revealed to the Cherokees a vision of the coming of these aliens and taught them the Booger Dance to deflect their contamination. In this ritual, men donned carved masks and performed a complex series of dances that often mocked the imported cultures, in an attempt to lighten the grief of their own oppression.

Although the Booger Dance is no longer performed, the tradition of maskmaking is still practiced by a handful of Cherokee men who handcarve the same snake masks, Caucasian, black, and Indian Booger masks and animal decoy masks that their ancestors made. One of these men, Will Long, is the last in a long line of mask carvers that at one time included his father, Allen Long, and his grandfather, Cherokee

Will Long's finished buckeye rattlesnake mask.

historian Will West Long.

He begins with a split buckeye log, the traditional wood for maskmaking. Supporting the split piece on another log, he studies it carefully. Then, without putting a single pencil mark on it, he begins to chip away at the exposed wood with a chisel and handmade mallet. Features begin to emerge, as if by magic. After completing the face, he hollows out the back, leaving a half-inch-thick wall.

In previous generations, the facial features on most of the masks were further exaggerated with hand-applied pigments made from red clay, pokeberries, black walnut hulls, butternut roots, and sumac berries. Today, commercial watercolors are used on some and others are left unpainted, finished simply with oils to allow the velvet-soft patina of the buckeye to show.

The rich symbolism and ceremony of the mask-maker's art have been lost, and despite its vitality, Will Long's work remains only a remnant of the tradition. It seems tragic that no one in Mr. Long's family is interested in continuing this ancient craft, nor are many members of the community.

Oil-finished buckeye wolf mask.

Painted buckeye booger mask.

Painted buckeye booger mask.

Oil-finished buckeye booger mask.

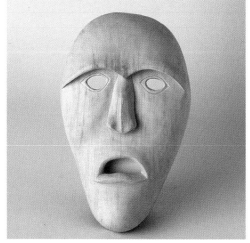

Oil-finished buckeye booger mask.

Stained buckeye bull mask.

Booger masks such as this painted buckeye example were worn at Cherokee ceremonial dances generations ago.

BROOMMAKING

A broommaker's tools rest on a workbench strewn with the scraps of broomcorn trimmed from the ends of a freshly made broom.

Spring, summer, and early fall were devoted to working the land in the early American settlements. During the cold months of late fall and early winter, however, the farmers became craftsmen and spent their time making and repairing the tools and equipment needed to sustain their existence. Broommaking was one of those essential pioneer crafts, practiced by nearly every rural household, using whatever plant materials were at hand. Round bundles of switches or sticks were tied to handles of

hickory to make besoms, now commonly referred to as witches' brooms. Wide, flat pieces of wood were bored with holes and then tightly filled with thinly stripped corn shucks to make sturdy mops. For many generations, almost any strong plant that was found growing near a homestead was gathered, bound to long handles, and used for cleaning chores.

One elderly North Carolina mountain woman, whose husband still makes delicately shredded but sturdy brooms from buckeye saplings, recalls the efficiency of this handmade cleaning equipment. "In those days, about once a week, the women would carry out everything they had, and they would scrub those cabins down. They'd take wood ashes and sand from along the creek, and dip those brooms in the hot water and scrub the floors. You see, the sand acted as an abrasive, and the ashes were like lye soap. The water would run right through the cracks in the floor. And those floors would be just as white as they possibly could be."

The introduction of broomcorn to this country from India, often attributed to Benjamin Franklin in the late 1780s, turned broommaking into an industry. Belonging to the same plant family as sorghum and millet, broomcorn was cultivated throughout the South and became the staple of a broommaking industry in many communities, among them the Shakers in Kentucky.

Like Shaker architecture and furniture, the crafts of this group expressed a beguiling simplicity, a high standard of excellence, and a genius for innovation. The Shakers are credited with many contributions to the craft of broommaking, including the systematic cultivation of broomcorn; the invention of vises and cranks used by the broommaker to hold, tie, and stitch the brooms; and finally, the invention of the now standard flat broom arriving at the turn of the twentieth century, which was a welcomed improvement over the less efficient, round broom.

The tradition of making brooms by hand from carefully grown and prepared broomcorn gradually diminished until, by the mid-1950s, it had all but been eliminated by machine-made products. Less sturdy than their handmade forebears, mass-produced brooms are made from synthetics or from imported broomcorn that is subjected to a process of bleaching and dyeing that destroys the natural strength and dust-collecting texture of the fibers. Their low cost, however, threatened to make handmade brooms a relic of the past.

Today, fortunately, the craft of broommaking is beginning to show evidence of a comeback. There are more and more people throughout the South who would not think of setting up a household without a "real" broom, and they are returning to the handmaking techniques of the past. The brooms they create—from home-grown broomcorn, buckeye saplings, twigs and grasses, and even palm trees—are more flexible and longer lasting than the commercial variety. More importantly, perhaps, they evoke an ineffable satisfaction in the hearts of those who own and use them.

BROOMCORN BROOMS

Since its introduction to this country, the easily grown and harvested broomcorn, a relative of the common sorghum plant, has maintained its dominance as the leading material for broommaking. Because of the high labor costs required to harvest the crops by hand, most broomcorn used commercially today is imported. There are still people in the South, however, who plant a few rows with their annual corn crop for personal use or grow enough for a small commercial broom production.

One such broommaker is Paul Strader, who learned the craft from a neighbor in western Kentucky who was selling his equipment. Recalling his start a quarter century ago, Mr. Strader says, "I told him if I had a broom outfit and some seed, I might raise a bit. I've been making brooms ever since."

1. After the broomcorn is harvested and dried, it is divided into piles of varying lengths.

2. To begin a broom, Kentucky broommaker Paul Strader trims off the long ends of the broomcorn stalks before soaking them in water to make them pliable and more easily compressed.

After harvesting and drying his "straw," the tassels that grow from the top of the plant, Mr. Strader divides it into piles of varying lengths. "Putting the long straws on the outside and the shorter straws on the inside makes a fuller broom," he explains. The straws are soaked in water to make them pliable and more easily compressed, then laid against a wooden dowel attached to a treadle-powered wiring machine. He works the foot pedal to turn the dowel, adding more straw as the wire binds it, then slices off the tight fringe just above the wire, leaving the long, bushy straws below the wire to dry. Once they are dry, he clamps the brooms securely into a broom vise, which presses the straw out flat for him to sew.

Using a long strand of colored cotton cord and a heavy needle, he first pushes the needle through the straw, then circles the flattened straw twice with the cord. Next, he forces the needle back and forth through the flattened straw, catching the circled cord with stitches at one-inch intervals all the way around. He does two more rows the same way, then evenly trims off the ragged bottom edges of the broom.

3. *The stalks are laid against a wooden dowel and bound to it with wire.*

4. *After allowing the broomcorn to dry, Mr. Strader clamps the broom in his vise, flattening the straw. He then permanently shapes the broom into the characteristic flat shape by stitching it with strong cord.*

The small handcrafted whisk broom is durable enough to provide assistance for many years.

5. Paul Strader exhibits his freshly sewn broom. As a final step, he will trim off the ragged ends of the broom, leaving an even edge to sweep.

GROWING & HARVESTING BROOMCORN

Only a few feet of sunny space are required for growing broomcorn. This tall, hardy plant, with jointed stems resembling a cornstalk, can be planted in any area full of sun. Often topping out at more than ten feet with airy sprays of seed heads, broomcorn can, according to the Henry Field Seed Company catalog, "make an unusual privacy screen, and make perfect brooms that won't fray like the plastic ones do."

After the soil has been tested and fertilized, the seeds are planted four inches apart in rows that are thirty inches apart. (A plot of two ten-foot rows will yield enough broom straw for two to four average-sized brooms.) When the plants reach six inches tall, they are thinned out to twelve inches apart.

In late summer, about a hundred days after planting, the broomcorn will "head out," forming the tassels, or straws, that are used for the "sweep" of the broom. At this point, while the seed heads are still green, each plant must be crimped about three feet below the seed head and allowed to hang straight down. This process, called "tabling," helps the brush to remain straight as it dries. If the stalk is not turned down, the head, heavy with seeds, will become twisted and bent by wind and rain, and the broom straw will not be usable for broommaking. After several weeks of hanging this way, the "boot," the thick, corn-like leaves surrounding the stalk, will begin to turn yellow.

At this point the stalks can be cut, while the broom straw is still green, or they can be cut after several more weeks, when the seeds are fully ripe and the straw has turned a bright rust color. As the straw dries and darkens in color, however, it becomes more and more brittle and less easily worked into a broom. Therefore, for a sturdy broom, it is better to cut the stalks while the seed heads are still green, but for a decorative broom, the straw can be allowed to turn a darker color.

Once the straw has turned the desired color, the bent tassel and about two feet of stalk are cut from the plant. The stalks are stripped of their remaining leaves and left in the sun to cure on a screen or board. When the tassels are thoroughly dry and spring back when gently bent, they are ready to be made into brooms. All that remains to be done is trimming the stalks to the desired length and "seeding the heads" by combing the seeds out with a wide-tooth comb. (The seeds make great feed for winter birds.) If the stalks are not used immediately, they should be stored flat in a dry place to keep the broom straw straight.

If the broom straw is harvested while it is still green, the resulting broom will be strong and pliable. As the straw dries, it becomes more brittle.

SEDGE BROOMS

Sedge grass, often called broom sedge because of its use in the South as a popular broommaking material, has for generations been transformed from a common field weed into light, feathery brooms, perfect for cleaning cobwebs, sweeping under beds, and even working in the yard. Mallie Weathersby, who has been making sedge brooms for more than fifty years, recalls using these brooms every day in her southern Mississippi home. "People out in the rurals where I lived, they knowed the art. That's all we had to sweep with when I was growing up. We didn't know anything 'bout a stick broom!"

In the autumn, after the first frost, the sedge is harvested from the fields where it flourishes in lush, solid stands. In the past, whole families traveled to the sedge fields for the gathering. "It grew in those fields just like oats or wheat," Mrs. Weathersby remembers, "and moved in the wind like a big, golden wave. You didn't know which place to start cutting, it was all so beautiful." The sedge grass was gathered by the armload—pulled from the soil by hand or cut off with a knife at the base of the plant—and carted home to barns and sheds to be stored for the year's supply of brooms. The light, feathery brooms lasted only a few months and were made as needed.

Preparation of the stored sedge begins with shaking off the dried blossoms. "You just shake it, lay it out in the sun, turn it over, and shake it some more," Mrs. Weathersby says. "Pretty soon all those blooms fly away, just like bees!" Next, a handful of sedge stalks are laid across the lap and an old kitchen knife used to "shuck" them, scraping and making them smooth and free from the thin, sharp fibers along their lengths. The sleek stalks are then wrapped together with twine

1. Mississippi broommaker Mallie Weathersby "shucks" sedge stalks with an old kitchen knife to remove sharp fibers that might prick her fingers.

or rags, and the feathery top part of the sedge left to form the broom.

Mrs. Weathersby recalls the day her father altered the process by using rubber strips to wrap the sedge, creating a longer lasting broom. "Way back then, people didn't know 'bout cars. They went by horse and buggy, mule and wagon. After people got automobiles, they had inner tubes, and they found that those old inner tubes were good for a lot of uses. My daddy slit one up and made a broom and wrapped one up with it. He told the people in the community to get some rubber and wrap their brooms with it, and it would make them last longer and make them stouter than anything. After that, we went to using rubber. It really worked!"

Although no longer the only kind of broom available to her, sedge brooms continue to be Mrs. Weathersby's favorite for sweeping chores. She still gathers the fluffy sedge each year and makes the brooms for use around her own house, as well as "for the old shut-ins, who want them just to look at, to remind them of the old times."

2. After the stalks are completely smooth, Mrs. Weathersby wraps them tightly together with a narrow length of rubber.

3. The light, feathery part of the sedge is left free, making a perfect broom for simple chores.

PALMETTO BROOMS

In the warm coastal areas of the South, palmetto and other types of palms flourish, supplanting hardwoods as the dominant growth. Brooms can easily and quickly be made from their shredded fronds. Today palmetto brooms are produced by elderly members of the Houma tribe in southeastern Louisiana, primarily for decorative use. For many generations in the past, however, the Houma Indians used the frond brooms to sweep the dirt floors of their homes.

The Houmas harvest the palmetto in the same manner as for their braided basketry, choosing the fan shape from the center of the plant. Then they separate the fronds and lay them out on a window screen or hang them from a clothesline, where they are left to dry thoroughly in the sun.

The construction of a broom begins with a handful of dried fronds. From the top of the grouped fronds to about halfway down their length, they are lashed together tightly with twine, forming a handle. A short piece of palmetto stalk or wood, bored with a small hole for hanging the finished broom, is wedged into the lashed handle. At the splayed end, each frond is then delicately split into several pieces, from the bottom of the broom halfway up to where they have been lashed together. The resulting feathered palmetto splits are then flattened by hand and sewn with brightly colored yarn or cord into the familiar flat shape for sweeping.

As a finishing touch, the Houmas decorate the completed broom by wrapping the cord-encircled handle with a long, braided strand of palmetto, identical to the braided strands they use to make their braided palmetto baskets.

Along the warmer coasts of the South where palmetto abounds, the fronds of the plant are shredded and used to make sturdy brooms, which often sport decoratively braided handles.

BUCKEYE BROOMS

Isaac Davis, Broom Maker of Blue Lick, Kentucky, *ca. 1932, by Doris Ulmann.*

An ingenious, mop-like broom is made by some mountain broommakers from a single branch of buckeye. Shavings whittled from one end of the branch are left attached, then turned down and tightly bundled.

The abrasive, mop-like broom once used to clean the floors of log houses is still being made today by some mountain people in North Carolina. Small, straight buckeye saplings or branches two to three inches in diameter and about four feet long are cut "green" while the sap is still running. After the bark is removed, the bottom part of the pole is whittled into dozens of shavings, or "splits," each about a foot in length, and left attached to the pole above. Next, more splits are carefully whittled in the opposite direction from a point on the pole about twelve inches above the split ends and are also left attached. Finally, the shavings are soaked in water to make them pliable and the top splits bent down, covering the splits underneath. The whole group of splits is then bound together with a strip of hickory bark, and the broom is ready for scrubbing.

SPINNING, DYEING & WEAVING

Simple two-harness looms have for generations been used to produce textiles ranging from sturdy, utilitarian fabric to material fine enough to pass on as heirlooms.

As essential as the production of food or the maintenance of shelter, the textile crafts of spinning, dyeing, and weaving were practiced in all rural households. Although many early city dwellers near the coasts could rely on trade with England for their woolens, cottons, and linens, Southern women in the earliest homesteads, like their counterparts in the North, were likely to spin their own thread and weave their own cloth.

The processes were often laborious and time-consuming, first beginning with the growing and harvesting of the raw fibers, whether from the ground or the backs of an animal. Sheep were raised in the cooler, upper regions of the South, and cotton and flax were cultivated in other sections. Each year the sheep had to be sheared, the flax cut, and the cotton picked. To prepare the raw wool for spinning, it was picked over by hand to clean it of burrs, twigs, and dirt, carefully washed and dried, then "carded," or combed, to untangle and separate the long fibers. The flax was "retted" (soaked in water to separate the woody part of the plant from the fiber), "swingled" (beaten and scraped clean), and then combed. Seeds were picked from the raw "lint" of cotton bolls, and then the cotton was also carded to prepare it for spinning.

Before any prepared fiber could be woven, it had to be spun, which was by far the most time-consuming part of cloth production. Pioneer women spent so much time at their spinning wheels that the distaff, the shaft of wood on which the raw fiber is placed during spinning, became the symbol for women. (To this day, *distaff* refers to the maternal side of the family.)

The process of dyeing the yarn or thread was undertaken next. Rancid baths of crushed or shredded plants grown on the farm or harvested from the fields and woods were combined with urine to set the dyes. The soft, subtle range of colors included lavender from pokeberries, warm blacks and grays from walnut bark and shells, and yellow from sassafras flowers, among many others.

Weaving, mostly of sturdy, utilitarian cloth, was done on simple two- or four-harness looms. In some areas of the South, traveling weavers carrying large, portable looms were employed to weave a family's spun thread. Their textiles were more intricately patterned than the average farm wife could manage or bigger than she could produce on her smaller loom.

With only minor adjustments in technique, the textile crafts remained unchanged in the South until well into the late nineteenth century. But, as happened to many of the early crafts, change came suddenly. With the advent of manufacturing in the second half of the nineteenth century, the art of weaving was quickly turned into the industry of textiles. The increasing availability of inexpensive cloth made in the great textile mills of the North eliminated the need for home production. In the early 1800s, there were over 17,000 hand looms in operation in Tennessee alone. One hundred years later there were very few people left who could even name the parts of a loom, much less thread one.

Fortunately, in some of the more isolated Southern communities, the old textile traditions were never rendered completely extinct by factory-made products and could be resurrected during the crafts revival of recent decades. Because so many people today consider things made by hand from natural materials aesthetically more pleasing and environmentally more sound than manufactured items, hand spinning, vegetal dyeing, and hand weaving continue throughout the South in a manner unchanged for generations.

Natural Dyeing

While much of the population has been spoiled in recent years by the seemingly endless array of brilliant colors available through synthetic dyes, there are many people throughout the South who prefer the softer, more illusive spectrum produced by natural dyes.

Beautiful colors are possible with hundreds of plants and vegetable fibers found in Southern gardens, woods, and fields. Sumac berries produce tans and grays; mosses and lichens give a variety of greens; the roots and bark of the sassafras tree yield reddish-brown hues. Marigolds give a golden color; beets, pink; grapes, a lovely lavender. Yellow, the most widely found color in nature, can be obtained from a remarkable variety of sources, including onion skins, milkweed, lily of the valley leaves, and hickory bark. Sometimes a single plant will produce a range of different colors depending on which parts are used and when they are harvested. For example, goldenrod blossoms picked in full bloom yield a soft yellow; blossoms harvested after the first frost produce a yellow-tan color. And yellow-green results when the stems are included.

Most vegetal dyes require a mordant, or chemical bath, in addition to the dye bath to set the color in the fiber. Without it, most dyes would simply stain the yarn or fabric for a while and then wash out. Mordants also affect the final color of the fiber. Combined with different mordants, a single dye can produce a variety of colors. Onion skins, for example, when combined with the common mordant alum, produce a bright yellow color. Combined with iron sulfate, they yield a deep brown.

Natural dyeing requires dedication. The hunting, collecting, drying, preparing, and processing of dyestuffs entail a tremendous effort compared to the relative ease of picking a commercial dye from a color chart. Nothing can compare, however, to the alchemist's delight and sheer magic of watching a garden's lush palette being transformed into the inner glow of fleece, yarns, and fabric.

Fibers such as wool fleece can be dyed either before or after they have been spun into yarn.

Natural dyeing is rewarding because of the range of beautiful colors that come from a variety of plants. Although harvesting the dyestuffs is necessarily seasonal, drying the plants for later use allows the dyer to work year round.

Chemicals called mordants are added to the dyes to prevent them from fading and also to control the final hue.

RAG RUGS

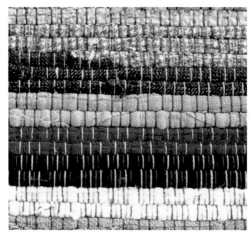

Rag rugmaking, often called a salvage craft, ingeniously transforms scraps of fabric into sturdy floor coverings.

Throughout the South, rag rugs are being woven today in exactly the same manner as they were hundreds of years ago. This salvage craft provides an ingenious way to use outgrown or worn garments or scraps of material from sewing projects.

In several North Carolina mountain communities, families living near the region's textile mills could help sustain themselves by weaving "loopers," rag rugs made from the circular pieces of material, or loops, that were discarded during the manufacture of socks. For generations entire families have knotted the loops together, wound the lengths around shuttles, and woven soft, absorbent rugs for sale. One local resident recalls that, in rugmaking families, not even the children were exempt from work. "In order to survive, everyone had to contribute."

North Carolina native Marilyn McMinn-McCrady learned to count at the age of three by looping for her grandmother. "She said, 'Now you have one here and one here. When you put them together, you have two. And one and one are two.' I can remember when I got past twenty. It was a terrific experience!"

Making loopers is still a thriving cottage industry in North Carolina, but it is no longer common for family groups to work together on the rugs. Instead, the various jobs in rug production are spread throughout the community. One woman, for instance, will receive the shipment of loopers, separate them by quality and weight, and dye them various colors. Another will then knot the individual circles together into long continuous lengths and roll them into balls. Yet another will wind the lengths onto shuttles and weave the rugs.

The thick, absorbent, and completely washable rugs are instantly appealing both to buyers living in North Carolina and to those who pass through the state on their way to other places.

(Right) *The weaving of soft, absorbent "looper" rugs is a thriving cottage industry in some North Carolina mountain communities.*

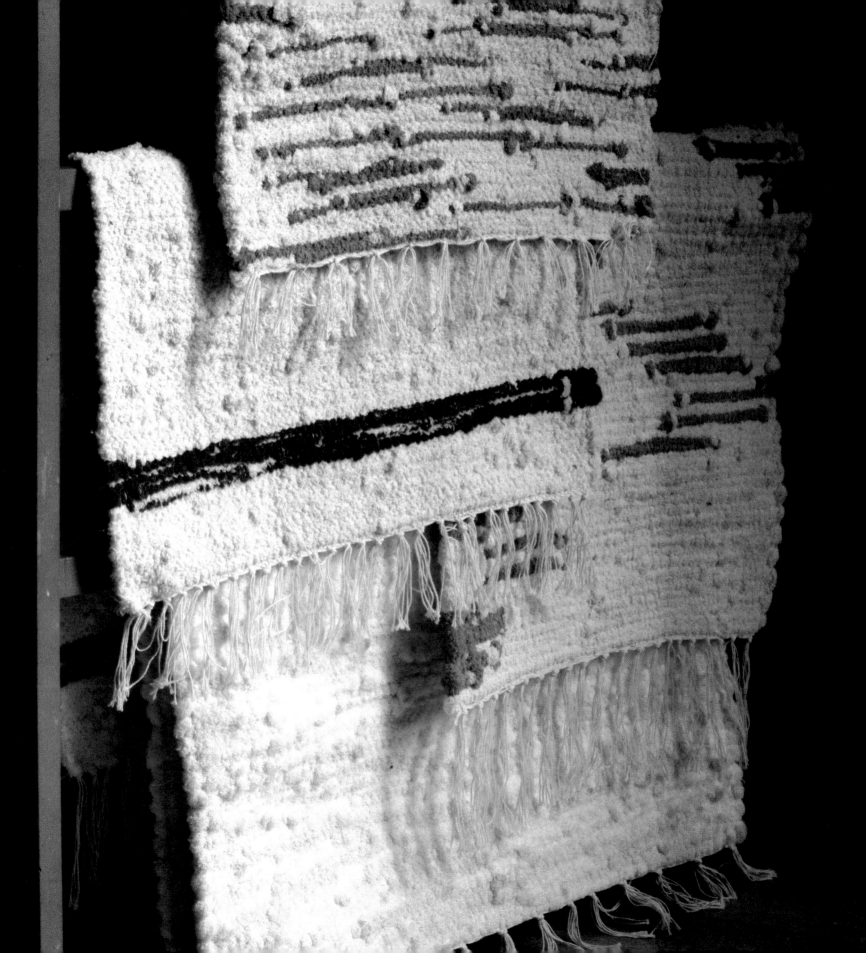

ACADIAN TEXTILES

The French ancestors of the Acadians emigrated to the French colony of Acadia, now known as Nova Scotia, in the beginning of the seventeenth century. Expelled from there in 1755, when the British gained possession of the region, many of the Acadian exiles found refuge in French colonial Louisiana, where they formed the largest single immigrant group. They settled in the Gulf Coast region and continued with their fishing, farming, and trapping lifestyles in a tradition so unique that to this day their descendants are still familiarly known as Cajuns.

Among the little they brought with them to Louisiana were their strong spinning and weaving traditions. Although they were accustomed to the cooler climates of France and Canada, where wool had been used to make textiles, they adapted to the different materials available in their new home, the most prevalent being

Acadian textiles, like the blanket under this basket, are traditionally woven of cotton on simple two-harness looms. Both white and brown cotton, shown here as just-picked bolls, have been cultivated for generations in Louisiana for spinning and weaving.

1. *Acadian weaver Gladys LeBlanc Clark first cleans the cotton "lint" of seeds, sticks, and burrs.*

2. *Next, she "cards" the lint, combing the fibers on the metal teeth of her paddles, called écartes.*

3. *After combing the lint back and forth from paddle to paddle, she rolls it into a roulée.*

4. *Mrs. Clark places the roulée in a basket and continues until she has enough to spin.*

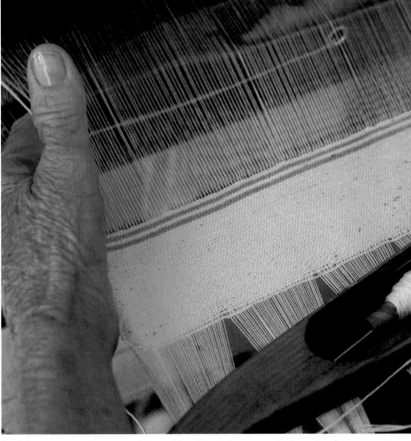

5. *As she feeds the soft cotton roll into previously spun thread, the fibers are twisted together.*

6. *After spinning for several days, Mrs. Clark has enough thread to begin weaving. With brown cotton on one shuttle and white on another, she builds up the length of her fabric thread upon thread.*

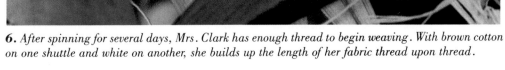

The result of many weeks' work, these hand towels, woven by Mrs. Clark from cotton she cultivated, carded, and spun herself, represent an unparalleled dedication to the craft of Acadian weaving.

cotton. The adjustment from wool to cotton occurred quickly.

Cultivated as a primary crop in Louisiana since the beginning of the eighteenth century, cotton was a particularly suitable fiber for bedding and clothing textiles. Light in weight, its tendency to absorb moisture—up to 65 percent of its own weight—and then release it slowly keeps the body cool even in the most subtropical climates. This feature makes cotton ideal for the Louisiana climate.

Perhaps the most distinctive characteristic of Acadian textiles was the use of *coton jaune*, or brown cotton, in addition to commercially grown white cotton. First found wild and then cultivated in small garden plots, it reminded the Acadians of their Canadian wools, which they had dyed brown with butternut and black walnut hulls. Ranging in color from a very light beige to a rich *café au lait*, the brown cotton quickly became an identifying characteristic of Acadian fabrics. These characteristics continue to distinguish Acadian textiles.

Much of the time and energy of the Acadian woman was devoted not only to the production of her family's clothing but also to a custom called *l'amour de maman*, "mother's love," which involved the creation of a staggering inventory of household linens for each child's trousseau. Although varying from household to household, a typical *l'amour de maman* might have included twelve *couvertures*, or blankets, which were assembled from two loom-widths of fabric and are the most plentiful of the Acadian textiles that have survived to the present. There would also be twelve *courtes-pointes*, coverlets or bedspreads assembled from three loom-widths of fabric; six *draps*, or sheets; four *paillasses*, mattress covers that were split and hemmed in various places to allow a stuffing of corn shucks or Spanish moss to be inserted later; covers for pillows;

and a variety of towels, quilts, and many other items that were considered essential for setting up a new household. With an average of ten children in each family, the labor required to produce such an array of textiles represented an unparalleled investment in the future of each new generation and became, in terms of the exhausting time and energy expended, the focal point of every family's life.

Creating plainly woven patterns on simple two-harness looms, with a palette limited to the natural colors of the brown and white cottons occasionally dyed blue with indigo, Acadian women produced a spectacular range of beautiful textiles. Textural variety in the simply woven fabrics was accomplished by inserting *cordons*, heavier warp or weft threads, into the pattern; by manipulating the weft thread into a *bouton*, or button-like nub of thread that stood out from the rest of the fabric; or by laying *chenilles*, short pieces of a heavier-weight thread such as rag scraps, along the weft as the fabric was woven. Bands of color were a common feature, sometimes the brown and white alone and other times the blue of indigo-dyed cotton as well.

The deep-rooted Acadian tradition of making textiles for home and family continued to be passed down from mother to daughter until the 1930s. Then, in a well-intended but doomed effort to foster continuation of the region's handicrafts as a means of livelihood, the Works Progress Administration found markets for the textiles outside the family structure. The shift in focus from the family to outside markets broke the tradition of *l'amour de maman*, and when the WPA program was discontinued, production diminished almost to the point of extinction. Today only a few people can recall the love and devotion that were lavished upon them through the handwork of their female ancestors.

One Acadian weaver who continues the textile tradition of working with *coton jaune* is Louisiana native Gladys LeBlanc Clark. She remembers learning how to spin and weave the brown cotton from her mother and recalls watching her produce *l'amour de maman* textiles for her children. "There were twelve of us. Mother had intended to give each of us our twelve blankets, so she carded and spun day and night." She completed trousseaus for the first five of her children, including Mrs. Clark, before she shifted to producing textiles for a market outside the home. Today Mrs. Clark continues to card, spin, and weave the cotton each day as her mother did.

The white cotton Mrs. Clark uses is commercially cultivated, but she plants a few rows of her own brown cotton each year and saves the seeds from each crop for the next year's planting. Since cotton requires one of the longest growing seasons of any Southern crop, she plants her seeds as soon in the spring as possible and harvests late in the fall.

After picking the bolls, or seed heads, from the stalks, she first removes the seeds and then laboriously cleans the mud, sticks, and burrs from some of the lint, or cotton fibers, by hand to use as a ready supply. She saves the rest of the crop and every few years takes a good-sized accumulation to a cotton gin in Alexandria, Louisiana. There the cotton is pressed between rollers to break up the "trash" in the lint, separated by metal teeth on a cylinder to loosen the fibers, and then blown apart from the loosened trash by an air blower.

Before the cotton can be spun into thread, it must be carded to separate and align the fibers. Using *écartes*, a pair of wooden carders or paddles with row upon row of tiny metal teeth imbedded in leather padding, Mrs. Clark first pulls a small handful of the cleaned lint evenly across one of the carders so that the fibers are caught in the metal teeth. Next she pulls the other carder gently across the lint with short stroking movements, separating the fibers. She works back and forth between the carders until the fibers are sufficiently pulled apart and then skillfully rolls the soft lint into a *roulée*, a soft, fat roll of cotton. She places the *roulée* in a basket and repeats the process until she feels that enough cotton has been carded for her to begin spinning.

Cotton is spun in essentially the same manner as wool, but because it has a shorter staple, or fiber, than wool, it must be handled more delicately to keep it from breaking while it is under tension during spinning. With a steady rhythmic beat, Mrs. Clark keeps the wheel spinning with a foot pedal while she carefully feeds the cotton roll into a previously spun leader thread. During spinning, the cotton fibers are alternately twisted together, making them stronger, and then drawn, or pulled out, to form a continuous strand of thread from the fluffy lint rolls.

After Mrs. Clark has spun for several days, she has enough thread to begin weaving. She "warps" her loom, threading it with enough commercially available cotton twine for several pieces that will be woven all at once, then later cut apart and fringed. After winding brown cotton on one shuttle and white on another, she starts to weave, raising one set of strings and then another, deftly passing her shuttle through each time and building up the length of her fabric, thread upon thread.

One of only a handful of Acadian weavers left, Mrs. Clark remarks sadly, "In my family, nobody's taking it up." The local weaver's guild, however, is helping to perpetuate the craft by instilling interest in younger weavers. For herself, Mrs. Clark plans no break from her traditions. "I do love to weave. I'll be at that loom or wheel just about every day!"

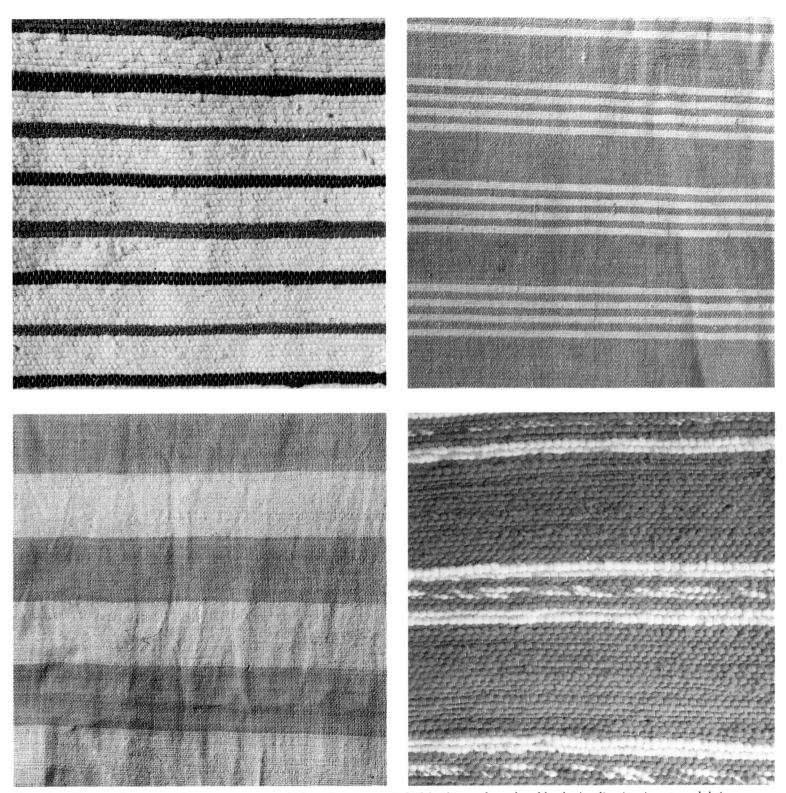

Examples of l'amour de maman, *these* couvertures, *or bedcoverings, are typical of the thousands produced by the Acadian immigrants and their descendants. Despite a simple weave and a palette limited to brown, white, and blue, they created a remarkable range of textures and patterns.*

NET WEAVING

and one end is sewn shut. Inside each cylinder, several "throats," or funnel shapes, are made from the knotted twine, with openings of decreasing diameter, through which the fish will pass once they have entered the net in search of bait. The fish become trapped in the last compartment of the net, unable to swim out through the small opening, and remain alive there until the net is "worked," or pulled from the water.

In previous generations, hoop nets were made of cotton twine and dipped in hot coal tar to preserve them, a process that had to be repeated every week or so. Now made of nylon, the nets are still tarred to keep them clean, to protect them from the

Kentucky fisherman Wade Grant, who lives along the Ohio River, uses a handcarved shuttle to weave his hoop nets.

Along the rivers, lakes, and bayous of the South, the creation of fish nets, often referred to as "net weaving," is still a practiced craft. Using nothing but a small shuttle and nylon twine, net weavers knot the twine into a variety of shapes, just as their ancestors have done for generations.

Hoop nets are among the most commonly used type of net in the South, especially along the Louisiana bayous. Knotted into twelve- to fourteen-foot-long cylinders, each is about four feet across. Wooden or fiberglass hoops are spaced at regular intervals along the length of the cylinders,

Louisiana fisherman Kaiser Dupuis repairs a hoop net made by his father, Herman Dupuis. This type of net, which is used to catch many varieties of fish, is especially common along the Louisiana bayous.

ravages of crustacean claws, and to darken them to deceive the fish. Nylon, however, makes retarring necessary only every four to six months.

The hoop nets are set along the bayous with the open ends facing downstream. Floats, such as empty plastic detergent and bleach bottles, used to be tied to the nets to mark their locations, but with the depressed economy in some parts of the South has come increased thievery. Most fishermen now either lay their nets without marking them or, at the most, make a little nick on a tree near the bank that no one will notice. With each fishing family setting as many as 200 nets out at a time and working 60 to 70 each day, the necessity of restricting their markings would seem to make their job more formidable. But Louisiana fisherman Kaiser Dupuis, speaking modestly about the difficulty of finding the meagerly marked nets, says, "It's not hard. After you've been on the river so long, you know every stump in the water."

Arthur Horton, also of Louisiana, has crawled through the funnel- shaped "throats" of his fourteen-foot hoop net to repair the end.

Metalworking & Leather Tooling

A blacksmith's tools rest on a wooden stump near his fire. Such implements have served the traditional ironworker since the earliest days of settlement.

The mining, refining, and manufacture of iron was an immense enterprise involving a wide variety of specialists, raw materials, products, and types and size of operation. The wrought iron produced as one facet of this enterprise was an essential part of the earliest settlers' personal inventory. When a blacksmith had not yet established a shop in a community, individual families would, themselves, carry ten or twenty pounds of the metal from their more settled homeland into the frontier. There they set up crude forges and hammered out the objects essential to their existence—kitchen tools, wagon wheels, hinges, and even nails to build their homes.

As frontier communities developed during the more than two centuries of expanding settlement, each village had its blacksmith, and his shop was the figurative hearth of the collective home. Directly affecting more lives than perhaps any other craftsperson, the blacksmith produced and repaired objects for the home and farm, from knitting needles to ox yokes. Those who practiced numerous other crafts depended on him as well to provide essential tools and supplies—barrel hoops for the cooper, horseshoeing tools for the farrier, wagon rims for the wainwright.

As large cities like New Orleans and Charleston evolved from earlier settlements, blacksmiths practiced the imported European tradition of more decorative and artistic uses for metal, producing gates, railings, and other ornamental architectural embellishments. Slaves were often apprenticed out to master metalworkers for several years at a time, then brought home to the plantation to continue their work at the trade. After the Civil War, many freed slaves continued to work for their former masters, who retained a large share of the produced income in exchange for providing the shop.

The pivotal role of the community blacksmith endured even into the twentieth century through the manufacture of farming equipment and the sharpening of plow points. But increasing industrialization from the mid-nineteenth century on hastened the severe reduction of the traditional blacksmith's trade. When tools broke, they were no longer repaired, but were replaced with new ones manufactured in factories. Cars replaced the buggy, eliminating the need for wheel rims and wagon fittings. Labor-

intensive farming was made easier by the introduction of the tractor, and soon there were no more plow points to sharpen. The introduction of gas welding equipment in the first part of the twentieth century made the slower, more tedious forge welding with hammer and anvil less attractive for a variety of tasks. The two world wars discouraged the use of iron for decorative purposes. And, finally, postwar architecture disdained the use of fancy metal adornment.

Unlike tinsmiths, coppersmiths, and bell-makers, whose trades all but vanished with the introduction of manufactured products, blacksmiths adapted to the market and survived through several generations by separating into three major specializations—the general metal repairers, who now use acetylene torches; the farriers, who continue to shoe horses in traditional ways; and the ornamental ironworkers, who, with minor changes to their shops, continue to work in the old ways, repairing the lacy ironwork produced a century ago, recreating old forms, and creating new ones.

Wherever you find horses, you'll find not only farriers, but saddlemakers as well, producing both utilitarian and highly decorative leather products. Together, the practitioners of the two trades maintain a working knowledge of craft traditions as old as this country.

FORGED METALWORK

The blacksmith's shop has changed very little in the last few centuries. The alternating glow and spark of the fire, the acrid aroma of burning coal, the music of the hammer striking the anvil, and the piercing hiss of red hot metal dunked into water to cool—all create the same sensory experience today that they did generations ago. Although the respect once accorded to blacksmiths as pivotal members of their communities has eroded through the years, there has been a recent revival of interest in blacksmithing. A growing number of ironworkers are learning the ancient techniques either by working with the few blacksmiths who have survived in the trade or by attending workshops in such places as the John C. Campbell Folk School in Brasstown, North Carolina. Today's new generation of smiths is creating objects ranging from kitchen hooks to elaborate iron grillwork, but the methods they use have not changed since colonial times.

The blacksmith begins each day by building the fire upon which the craft depends. Knowing how to build, maintain, and work the fire is one of the most vital and difficult skills to learn. The fire requires almost constant attention. The more air it is given, the hotter it burns, but if the flow of air to the fire stops, the fire dies. Metal that is worked too hot can spark uncontrollably, burning the smith's hands, but metal that is worked too cold can be weakened when hammered.

The fuel that most smiths prefer is "blacksmith's coal," a soft, bituminous coal that converts easily, after a short burning time, into lightweight and porous coke, the relatively pure, high-carbon material that is actually used to heat the iron. The smith starts a fire by filling the forge, the small furnace in which the iron is heated, with kindling under a layer of coal. The fire is fanned with air from a blower fan. As the coal burns and converts to coke, the smith mounds it into the center and banks it with fresh coal around the edges. By properly maintaining the air flow and carefully adding fuel, the smith will have a good fire that lasts to the end of the workday.

Blacksmith Glenn Gilmore's handmade tools were also hand-forged from steel, using techniques as old as the craft itself.

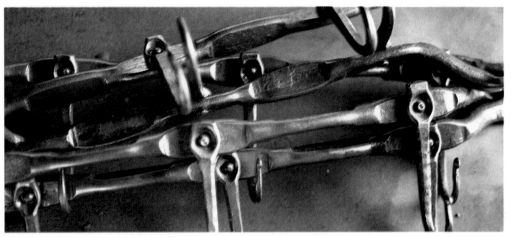

After being heated to cherry red, a steel rod is hammered and bent into a hook shape.

The blacksmith pierces a hole in the hook by hammering a punch onto the red-hot metal, then rivets several hooks to a steel frame to create a pot-hanging kitchen rack.

Traditional blacksmithing is taught at the John C. Campbell Folk school in Brasstown, North Carolina. Students work at their own forges.

To make a simple hook, the smith heats a foot-long piece of steel rod to cherry red in the fire and pushes and pulls it about in the heat with one of his many pairs of tongs. Removing it from the fire and quickly placing the heated portion on the anvil, the blacksmith begins to hammer the rod a few inches from the end, turning it over with each blow and "drawing out," or lengthening, the steel until it tapers to a point. The rod cools down during hammering and may require several "heats" before the tapering is completed. To make the bend of the hook, the smith pulls the rod from the fire once again and hammers the tapered point over the rounded horn of the anvil.

One way of joining two pieces of metal together is by forge welding, a method practiced since the earliest recorded days of ironworking. The two pieces to be joined are first heated to red hot, removed from the fire, and quickly sprinkled with flux, a material that aids in welding. The pieces are then reintroduced to the fire and heated to welding, or near white, heat. Working quickly, the smith removes the first piece from the fire, lays it on the anvil, and taps it to remove any impurities clinging to it that would prevent a solid weld. The second piece is removed, tapped, and placed in position on top of the first piece. With carefully placed hammer blows, the smith joins the two near molten pieces, creating a single piece of metal that, if properly welded, is as strong as its contributing parts.

The creation of beautiful objects from hot metal requires more than hammer blows, however. Other techniques, such as splitting, twisting, cutting, and even hot steel carving, are all part of the blacksmith's repertoire of skills. Building upon these long-established techniques, the contemporary ironworker invents new forms while also continuing to recreate historical objects.

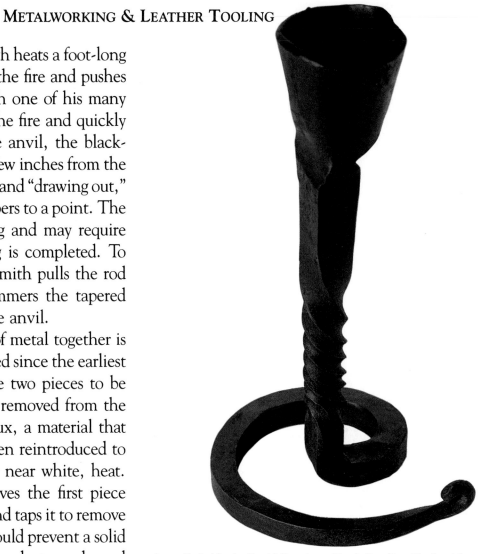

A candle holder by David Brewin, a North Carolina blacksmith, was forged from a single bar of steel. The stem was twisted while the metal was still hot.

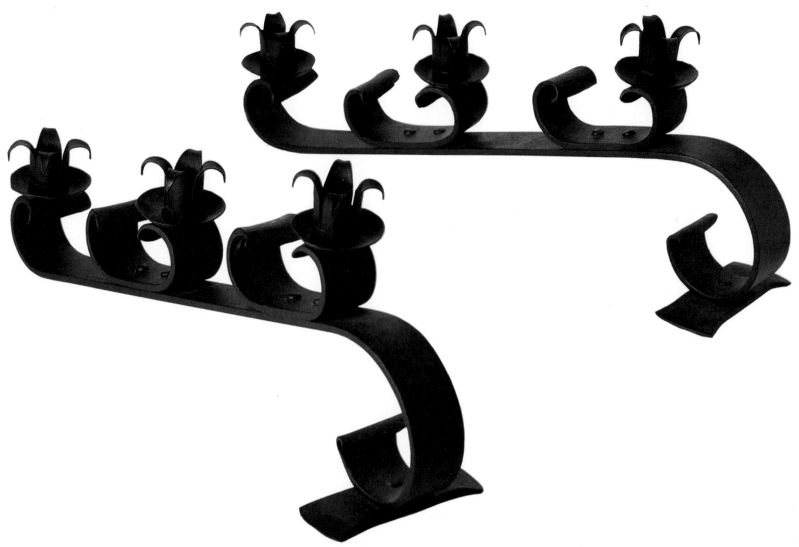

North Carolina blacksmith Oscar Cantrell forged a pair of candle holders from several pieces of metal, riveting and forge welding the pieces together. When properly done, a welded piece of metal can be as strong as its contributing parts.

Another single candle holder was made to be driven into the wall of a log cabin. It was photographed at a bird's eye view to better show the form.

HORSESHOES

While horseshoeing was only one part of the traditional blacksmith's work generations ago, it is now the specialized trade of the farrier. Working out of pickup trucks carrying small, portable forges, farriers travel from farm to ranch, practicing a trade that combines blacksmithing with animal husbandry skills and requires ease with horses, a strong back, and a good eye.

Bob Hollis, a Kentucky farrier, learned the fundamentals of his craft a decade ago during a twelve-week course of study at an Illinois horseshoeing school. After graduation, he moved to a farm in central Kentucky and placed an ad in the local paper announcing his farrier services. Since that time, the demand for his

shoeing has been so great that he typically works a six-day week, often traveling to as many as six different places in one day and putting more than 40,000 miles on his pickup each year. Bob sees the spread of miles from job to job as an advantage. "When I go from one job to another, it gives me a chance to rest. It's not the easiest job in the world, being bent over some smelly old horses all day!"

Most of his time is spent trimming and shoeing hundreds of horses, which must be done every three to six weeks. A typical day might include working on race and polo horses on a thoroughbred farm, a trail horse for a pleasure rider in the suburbs, old Shetland ponies for some farm children, and even working hand-in-hand with a vet to create corrective shoes for

1. Kentucky farrier Bob Hollis travels hundreds of miles from farm to ranch each day, carrying a portable forge in the back of his pickup truck. Setting up, complete with roaring fire, takes him only minutes.

2. *He first inspects the horse's feet to check the wear of the old shoes. Then he removes them, along with the old nails, and trims back the growth on each hoof.*

3. *He examines the old shoe; if it is too worn, he begins fresh with a new shoe.*

4. *After stoking the coals in his portable forge, he heats the shoe until the metal glows red with heat.*

5. *He moves the shoe about in the fire with his tongs to heat it evenly until it is malleable.*

6. *Working quickly while the shoe is still hot, he hammers it into shape on his anvil.*

7. *While the shoe is still hot, he carefully burns an impression on the bottom of the hoof, ensuring a good fit when he nails it on after it has cooled.*

a lame or ill-stepping horse.

Moving with incredible speed, he first inspects the horse's hooves to check the wear of the shoes before removing them along with the old nails. After trimming down each hoof, he examines the old shoe to see if it can be "reset," or used again. If it is too worn, he begins with a new shoe. After heating the shoe in his portable forge, he removes it from the fire with his tongs and corrects the fit by hammering it out on his anvil. Then, while the shoe is still hot, he carefully burns the shoe's impression on the bottom of the horse's hoof to create a good "seat," or fit. He lets the shoe cool while he works on the next hoof and then secures the shoe to the horse's newly trimmed hoof with six to eight nails. After an hour or so, Bob completes the four shoes and is on his way to the next horse.

His brother, John Hollis, also works with iron as an ornamental blacksmith, but Bob sees few similarities in their professions. "There's a lot more to the ornamental work than what I have to do," he modestly explains. "Basically, I just want heat, and it's pretty much cut and dried—bend this, bend that, cut this, rasp that."

WAGON WHEELS

efore World War I and the introduction of the horseless carriage, the wheelwright had a thriving business in almost every community, producing metal-rimmed tires for buggies and carriages and often even doubling as the village wainwright, creating the vehicles himself. Today, thanks to the revival of interest in carriage driving as a sport and an increase in the popularity of horse-drawn carriages as big city tourist attractions, the traditional wheelwright's skills are once again being called into more widespread use.

Factories still producing wagon wheels use a cold technique for "tiring" the wooden wheel with metal bands, but most contemporary wheelwrights prefer the old method of "sweating on a tire." The metal tire band is heated before being hammered onto the wooden rim, then doused with water to shrink it and permanently tighten the wheel.

Mississippi wheelwright O. D. Todd checks the fit of his metal tire on a wooden carriage wheel before "sweating" it on the rim.

SPURS

Along with boots, hat, and horse, spurs have become a distinct symbol of cowboy culture. Made in earlier days by village blacksmiths or even by the cowboys themselves, spurs were most often unadorned, utilitarian, and simply made, using such things as old buggy axles, car springs, or parts of threshing machines. The increasing number of professional rodeos and the popularity of movie and television westerns, however, have elevated the craft, and the contemporary spurmaker has become a cross between farrier and jeweler.

Steve Fredieu, a Texas spurmaker, produces the majority of his work for active cowboys who work with cutting horses. "The spurs are used every day, and used hard," Mr. Fredieu explains. "The cowboys put 'em on and are in them twenty-four hours a day, if they're up twenty-four hours a day."

Fashioned from high-carbon tooled steel, many of the spurs are overlaid with silver or gold and sometimes inlaid with precious stones. Construction of a spur begins with the heel band, a U-shaped metal band to which the spurs are attached. To save time, it is initially formed with a metal press. The remainder of the work—the final shaping and fitting of the band and the construction of the shank and the spoked rowel—is done by hand using a hammer and anvil. Each pair is precisely fitted to the wearer's boots.

Despite the attraction of highly embellished ornamental spurs, the working cowboy values his spurs less for their decoration than for their aid in directing his mount. When a cowboy is "cutting" cattle, or separating them from the herd, he doesn't use the reins to control his horse but relies on body movement and the action of his spurs to communicate with his horse.

Texas spurmaker Steve Fredieu creates his basic spur shapes from high-carbon tooled steel, then embellishes them with overlaid gold and silver and sometimes even inlaid precious stones.

Despite the highly decorated appearance of the spurs, the working cowboy values them less for ornamentation than for their aid in directing his horse.

SADDLES

Before the advent of the automobile, when horses were the chief mode of transportation, the demand was high for craftspeople who could produce saddles, harnesses, and other required gear. Travel by horse is still preferred by many, including both pleasure riders and the ranchers who tend cattle over vast areas of open rangeland. Although much of the tack used by today's riders is factory-made, there remain several fine-quality saddlemakers in the South who use traditional hand methods to produce both utilitarian and elaborately embellished saddles.

Every saddle begins with a "tree," the foundation on which the saddle is built. Although factory-made saddles are built on mass-produced trees of laminated wood or fiberglass, most hand saddlers prefer to use handmade trees. Oscar Carvajal, Jr., a fourth-generation Texas saddlemaker, explains, "A good saddle has to start with a straight, true tree, preferably made of wood and covered with rawhide. Without that foundation, no matter how good the saddlemaker is, he

hasn't produced a good saddle."

One craftsman still producing one-of-a-kind trees is Texan Sam Adams, who begins with hand-picked white pine. First he rough cuts the four basic parts of the tree on a duplicating lathe—the two bars that span the horse's backbone and distribute the rider's weight evenly across the horse's back; the swell for the front end; and the cantle for the back—and then he sands them smooth. After the pieces are assembled into the tree, he wets pieces of rawhide, which he has cured himself, stretches them over the wooden tree, and sews them tightly with handmade rawhide lacing. As the rawhide dries, it shrinks and conforms exactly to the contours of the tree, producing a foundation that has steel-like strength. "Man hasn't made any fiber yet that can replace the combination of wood and rawhide," he boasts. "The wood is really strong in its own right, and then, with the rawhide on, there's just enough give. Each time you put a sudden stress on it, why, it'll retract right back!"

Using a tree such as the ones Sam Adams makes,

For an ornate parade saddle, Texan Oscar Carvajal, Sr., outlined the pattern with a swivel cutter.

Boo LeDoux uses a draw gauge, with the help of his wife, Priss, to cut strips of leather for lacing.

Although most factory-made saddles are built today over synthetic trees, good saddlers prefer handmade wooden trees like the one produced by Texan Sam Adams.

He sews sheepskin to the underside of the saddle seat, providing a comfortable fit for the horse.

Mr. LeDoux even makes his own loops through which the various saddle belts will pass.

Boo Le Doux hand stitches his saddle with durable waxed linen thread. Working in Louisiana, he has developed a reputation for his fine handmade saddles.

A saddle by Texas saddlemaker Gary Oden shows the incredible realism that hand-tooling can produce.

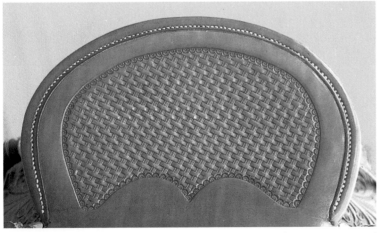

Gary Dunshee, like most saddlemakers, "cases" his leather, wetting it and then letting it dry almost completely, before he tools it into a basket weave.

Oscar Carvajal and his brother, Ernest, begin saddle construction by filling in the gap between the bars of the tree with sheet metal. Then they laminate four layers of leather over that, "skiving," or carving, into the thickness to form the cup of the seat. The sides are narrowed so that the rider's legs are not spread too wide, and the layers of leather are feathered and blended together.

After this groundwork is completed, the rest of the basic saddle is added. The horn and back cantle are covered; the skirts, seat, and back riggings are attached; and the stirrups added. Because the leather must be worked wet, and each step must be completely dry before proceeding to the next, a single saddle might take several weeks to produce.

Hand tooling, a craft for which the Carvajals are renowned, is a time-consuming decorative treatment frequently added to the production of saddles. The Carvajals begin a design by marking the leather with a soft pencil in a freehand pattern. Then, using a swivel knife, they cut the outline of the design into the leather. This outline is used as a guide for a wedge-shaped tool called a "shader," which is driven into the incision in continuous intervals with a rawhide mallet. The shader opens up the cut line and compresses the leather, turning the simple incised design into a remarkable display of three-dimensional leaves, flowers, and stars.

These hand saddlers, while creating beauty in their leatherwork, always stress that their saddles are made to be used. The saddlers strive for comfort for both the horse and the rider. "There are two things a cowboy likes," Oscar Carvajal explains. "A good pair of boots, and a good, comfortable, strong, working saddle. If a rider works all day, he may switch to a fresh horse at midday, but he's on that saddle all day, so it had better be comfortable!"

POTTERY
&TILEMAKING

For hundreds of years, since the discovery of natural clay deposits by the early settlers, Southern traditional potters have been "turning" and "burning" functional ware. Many of these same forms are still being produced today.

During the early nineteenth century, pottery manufacture was an important handcraft industry throughout the South wherever natural clay deposits were present, and especially in central North Carolina and northern Georgia. As the number of early settlers increased, so did the demand for utilitarian pottery. Staples of the typical Southern diet—salt-cured meats, molasses, milk products, lard, vegetables, whiskey—were processed, stored, preserved, and served in churns, jugs, crocks, pitchers, and "dirt dishes," so called because of their earthen origin. Working in small shops under difficult conditions and using only local raw materials, potters turned clay into sturdy vessels their neighbors could use. Little thought was given to decoration.

Pottery was generally made by specialists, as the construction and firing of a hot kiln were too exacting for the needs of an individual family. Even so, most of the hundreds of potters listed on the census rolls as turners or "jug makers" devoted their time primarily to farming and worked off-season at the pottery trade. Most of the labor in pottery shops was actually supplied by family members. Children were put to work at an early age driving a mule around the clay-mixing mill or helping to unload the wood-fired kilns after the wares had cooled. As they grew older and stronger, they dug clay from the local clay pits or chopped wood for the kiln fire. By the age of sixteen, they took their places at the wheel to turn the clay alongside older members of their families. The pieces that were not sold to neighbors were traded to the general stores for food, clothing, or fuel or driven by wagon to neighboring towns for sale.

The self-reliant, agrarian lifestyle of Southern potters helped preserve their craft traditions until well after the turn of the century, when inexpensive factory-made products began to appear in homes. People became increasingly dependent on commercial dairies, and so their need for churns and storage vessels dwindled. Prohibition severely reduced the need for whiskey jugs, and improved transportation and refrigeration methods diminished the demand for pickling and preserving crocks. Finally, World Wars I and II provided the opportunity for many young potters to leave their communities. By the 1950s, Southern ceramics had changed considerably.

Despite family potting traditions that spanned generations, many potters could not adjust to the variations in the market and closed their doors in the 1930s. But some moved their shops to more traveled roads, taking advantage of the burgeoning tourist industry. They expanded their repertoire to accommodate the demand for more decorative ware, which was designed to be visually appealing as well as useful. Old forms were given new functions—churns became planters, chamber pots became casseroles. And although many potters continued using local materials, they acquired labor-saving machinery that enabled them to produce more with less backbreaking labor.

Despite the changes in methods and materials, today's products are linked by form and technique to the past. The few family-operated potteries remaining still produce the traditional shapes—the jugs, the kraut jars, the deep, fluted pie plates. Potters still turn their wares by hand, using many of the old methods developed and refined by preceding generations. Many continue to dig their own clay, and a few still fire their wares with wood in homemade groundhog kilns. Among those who continue to make pots, there remains a universal respect for their materials. And among those who buy, there is respect for the potter's ability to fashion a beautiful object from a lump of clay.

STONEWARE

Stoneware pottery, aptly named, is distinguished by its high-fired, hard, and durable surface. Although it is frequently regarded as the only type of pottery produced in the South, the manufacture of stoneware was actually not possible until the discovery of large stoneware deposits in North Carolina in the first half of the eighteenth century. Prior to that, the only clay available for pottery in what are now the Southern Atlantic states yielded a soft redware, similar to today's flowerpots.

Early redware pots were made by English and German potters who settled in America in the early nineteenth century and used the similar red clay to duplicate the forms of the old country. They used clear glazes on the redware, most of which was left undecorated, except for the pottery of the Moravians. This group of German immigrants used colored slip (clay mixed with water to the consistency of heavy cream) to paint or apply designs to their pots before glazing them.

By the middle of the nineteenth century, stoneware had universally replaced the inferior early redware. Stoneware deposits, and consequently the production of pottery using this clay, centered on two areas of North Carolina, one in the Catawba Valley along the western Piedmont and the other in the Seagrove area.

The glazes used on early Southern stoneware distinguished it most obviously from pottery produced elsewhere. The simple one-coat salt and ash glazing techniques, although later used in ceramic workshops across America, were first introduced to this country in the South.

Salt glazing originated in Germany in the fifteenth century and from there spread to England before

Swirlware, or striped ware, popular in the western Piedmont area of North Carolina, is produced by combining light and dark clays before turning the pieces on the wheel.

migrating to America. In this technique, the dry, unglazed pots are placed on the floor of the kiln, whose temperature is then brought up to white heat. While the kiln is still firing, common table salt is thrown into the kiln, where it instantly vaporizes and bonds with the sand in the clay, forming a coating of glass on the exposed surfaces of the pots.

Because the early potters conserved kiln space by stacking their pieces closely together, the salt vapors often did not reach the interiors of the pots, which were left unglazed. This problem was solved in the late nineteenth century by the introduction of a slip glaze from Albany, New York. Albany slip, which adheres evenly to the pot, forms a smooth, brown surface when fired. It is still used today by many potters as an interior coating for salt-glazed ware, sealing the pots and making them easier to clean.

Unlike the imported salt-glazing technique, ash or alkaline glazing, also characteristic of early Southern stoneware, was entirely indigenous to the South. A basic mixture of ashes, clay, and sand is mixed with enough water to form a creamy solution. The unfired pots are dipped into this liquid and their bottoms wiped free of glaze. Before firing, the pots are thoroughly air dried.

Because the materials used in ash glazes change locally throughout the South, the final appearance of the pottery also varies. The glossy, usually transparent surfaces of the pots range in color from green to brown, depending on the amount of iron in the clay. Additions and substitutions to the basic glaze mixture—slaked lime, glass, marble dust, and even epsom salts—add to the colorful array. The glazing formulas are many, and the colorful names of the glazes—such as tobacco spit and frogskin—reflect the final appearance of the ware.

Among the remaining folk potters in the South,

The absence of decoration on this salt-glazed jug reflects the folk potter's attention to the function of utilitarian ware rather than its ornamentation.

Burlon Craig is typical in that he continues to work his stoneware with the methods he learned as a boy. Born in 1914, he first worked in the pottery industry grinding clay for a neighbor, using his father's mule. Although a tractor now powers his pug mill, he still digs his own clay, nearly six tons at a time, from bottomland near the Catawba River in North Carolina, an area that has provided clay to generations of pottery turners.

Before the excavated clay is ready to use, it is hauled back to a bin near his shop where it weathers for a year, its plasticity increased by the seasonal cycle of freezing and thawing. During this seasoning, the clay eventually dries out and must be soaked in water before it is mixed with rotating knives in the barrel-shaped pug mill. After grinding in the pug mill, the now workable clay is stored under moist burlap.

To create a pot, Mr. Craig takes a manageable amount of the stored clay and kneads it to further improve its workability. Picking out any small stones that remain, he forms the clay into a ball and centers it on his foot-powered treadle wheel. From this shapeless

(Left) Contemporary and antique salt-glazed jugs from North Carolina show a remarkable similarity in the work of many different potters.

mass, he creates both the graceful and the grotesque forms for which he is known, leaving them to dry on the shelves of his shop.

To produce his smooth ash glaze, Mr. Craig grinds bottles and windowpane glass between rocks until they are the consistency of flour, then adds wood ashes, water, and more clay to hold the mixture together. He dips the dry, unfired pieces into this solution and leaves them to dry a second time.

Four times each year, he "burns," or fires, as many as six hundred of his pieces in a traditional groundhog kiln, placing each piece directly on the sand floor of the kiln. Unlike some pottery, which is fired once for the pot and again for the glaze, Mr. Craig's pots are fired only once. Reaching temperatures around 2,400 degrees Fahrenheit, the glass in the glaze melts and fuses with the clay, forming a shiny, reflective surface on each piece. He occasionally sets pieces of broken glass on the rims of the pots, which melt in decorative streaks down the sides during firing.

Through the years, Burlon Craig has turned many different types of ware for the local market—churns, bean pots, bowls for feeding rabbits, waterers for chickens—but more recently he has become known for his

Ash-glazed, or alkaline-glazed, pieces derive their color from iron in both the clay and glaze.

tradition in the Southern pottery industry. Probably first created as novelties, an escape from the weary repetition of utilitarian potterymaking, face jugs remain a popular staple in the repertory of Burlon Craig and other Southern potters.

For nine generations, the Cole family has been turning pottery in North Carolina, and with three family shops still in operation, the tradition remains strong. One of the shops, Cole Pottery in Lee County, is run by two sisters, Celia and Neolia Cole, whose father began firing the first kiln load of ware in his own shop on the day Neolia was born in 1927. Although they no longer fire with wood, they still dig their own clay from a vein in Smithfield that has been mined by

Burlon Craig stands with one of his face jugs, which he will allow to dry completely before coating with a homemade glaze and burning in his groundhog kiln.

snake and face jugs. Today much of his work is finding its way into the homes and the shops of collectors and dealers.

Face jugs, also known as voodoo, grotesque, and ugly jugs, have been made by Southern potters since before the Civil War. Contrasting materials, such as broken china fragments for teeth and white clay for protruding eyes, are used to create exotic and often monstrous effects. Although there is no conclusive link between Mr. Craig's face jugs and the African forms they often resemble, they are a part of a long

Charles Lisk combined dark and light clays to produce a striking face jug.

their family for more than fifty years.

Many of their glaze formulas were handed down through the family, and their forms and shapes are reminiscent of pots made by their ancestors. The Cole sisters are perhaps best known, however, for the messages they incise on the bottoms of their pots: "Love you"; "Morning low temperature 40 degrees. Broke a record at Raleigh-Durham airport." These expressions reflect events in the sisters' lives and often relate directly to the function of the pieces themselves. The underside of a large bowl, for example, reads: "Let me help you with your party. Just don't spike the punch too much!"

The J.B. Cole Pottery, also in Lee County, was founded by Jacon Cole, a distant cousin of Celia and Neolia Cole, in the early 1920s. Jacon's son, Waymon Cole, had already been turning pottery for more than a decade at his father's shop when he was featured, along with his sister, Nell, in their 1932 catalog. "I have made pottery all of my life," declared his father in the pamphlet, "and so did my father before me. Then I taught my son and daughter, whom you see at their

A long tradition in Southern pottery, face jugs have been made primarily for the tourist and collector for the past fifty years.

Ninth-generation potter Celia Cole turns miniature versions of traditional ware using clay dug from the family clay pit.

wheels." Even in his eighties, Waymon works daily at the wheel, along with his sister and younger members of the family.

Up to eight tons of stoneware clay are dug once a year from the family pit near Raleigh and hauled back to an open shed at their shop. It is prepared for use in a big ball mill, a rotating barrel that contains tough, fist-sized porcelain balls that grind the clay to a fine texture.

In order to maintain consistency of form in any design, Waymon weighs the prepared clay, then uses a pointed, wooden gauge to mark the height while turning the clay on the wheel. The Cole pottery made in his workshop is glazed in a range of clear, luminous colors, some of which were originally developed by Jacon during the early wood-burning years and adapted to the oil-fueled kilns used since the 1950s to burn the ware.

Having worked in the pottery shop all his life, Waymon Cole still welcomes visitors, inviting them to watch the family produce their kitchenware and table-ware, vases and planters. "I like to do it," he says. "It's just a part of me. If I did any other kind of work, I'd go fishing tomorrow!"

The Cole sisters learned their turning techniques from their father, Arthur Cole, and they continue to this day producing the spongeware and spatterware for which he was known.

The Cole sisters' bowls are graceful and finely crafted, yet sturdy enough for everyday use.

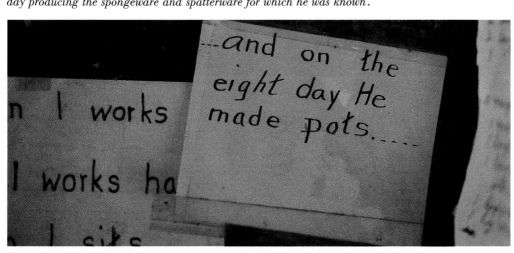

The sign hanging in Waymon Cole's North Carolina shop is testament to the production potters' dedication to their trade.

"Hot and humid today. High 95. Hello world. Love you" reads the base of a Cole bowl.

In this two-step process, the ware is first bisque-fired, then glazed and burned once more at higher temperatures.

Now in his eighties, Waymon Cole works at his wheel daily. The pointed gauge allows a quick check of height, providing consistency in his work.

Mugs made by Mr. Cole from clay dug from a pit near Raleigh, North Carolina, have changed little from those made by his predecessors.

GROUNDHOG KILN

Mouth of Eddie Averett Kiln, ca. 1927. A young boy unloads "monkey jugs," glazed at their tops with brown Albany slip, from the mouth of the groundhog kiln after the ware has been burned and cooled.

At the heart of any pottery workshop is the kiln, where pieces are fired, or "burned," as the final step in their production. The prevalent kiln in the South until the latter part of the nineteenth century was the groundhog kiln, so named for its shape, which resembles the animal's burrow. This type of kiln, still used by a few Southern potters, is essentially a wood-burning furnace in which the flame passes over a long, broad platform to a chimney at the rear.

Groundhog kilns are arched and rectangular in form. They typically measure sixteen to twenty feet long, six to eight feet wide, and only four feet high at the top of the arch; their chimneys average ten feet in height. Because they are fueled with wood, and the fire's heat must travel from the firebox at one end across the length of the kiln to the chimney, the temperature is hard to control. Packing the kiln is also difficult because the inside dimension of the loading area is only three feet high at its tallest point. The advantage of the kiln, however, is that it can be easily constructed with only basic tools and locally produced materials.

To prepare the kiln for burning a load of ware, the sand floor is smoothed and raked clean. Excess glaze is scraped off the bottom edges of the pots to prevent them from sticking to the sand during firing. Loading often takes the better part of a day. Crawling in and out of the kiln on hands and knees, the potter starts at the chimney end and laboriously fills the chamber. After stacking his firewood in the space reserved for it in front of the last pots, he constructs a temporary fire wall of

This groundhog kiln, still in operation, is loaded with ware several times a year and burned for many days. The flames pass over the pots from the fire box in the front to the chimney at the rear.

brick, sealing in the pots and first load of fuel.

To prevent sudden changes in temperature from cracking the pots, the wood fire is built up slowly for several hours and then increased for four to five hours with intermittent stokings of scrap pine slabs. As the temperature in the kiln approaches white heat, near 2,000 degrees Fahrenheit, the kiln is "blasted off" for several hours with constant stokings of wood. Red flames shoot across the ware and leap from the chimney at the far end. If the ware is to be salted, openings are left in the arch or the walls during blasting, and salt is thrown in when the fire is hot enough to vaporize it.

After the final stoking, the kiln is sealed once again and allowed to cool down gradually, the entire process having taken two to three days and two to three cords of wood. Finally, the ware is "drawn," or unloaded from the kiln, often to crowds of purchasers who have gathered in anticipation of buying a face or snake jug, some swirl ware, or simply a traditional piece to replace their broken jugs or crocks.

EARTHENWARE

The Cherokee and Catawba Indians also have a long and distinguished history of pottery manufacture. The earthenware used by these Native American tribes can still be found in the South. The clay is dug from pits near the surface of the earth and fired at a much lower temperature than stoneware clay. Pottery made from earthenware clay is formed by hand, polished with stones, and pit fired with wood.

Sara Ayers, a member of South Carolina's dwindling Catawba Indian tribe, practices the potterymaking skills that she learned as a child from her mother, using tools left to her by her grandmother. She blends together two types of clay found near the same river from which her people have been collecting clay for hundreds of years. After rolling the clay out into long coils, she winds them up layer upon layer to build her pots. While the coiled shape is still damp, she scrapes the sides with a mussel shell, then burnishes the surface with her polishing stone.

Before firing the pots in the traditional open pit, she gradually warms them in her kitchen oven to help prevent their cracking later in the fire. After heating them through, she places the pieces on an open pit of coals that have been reduced from three successive fires and covered with wood chips.

Several members of the Eastern Band of the Cherokee Indians are also continuing the pottery tradition of their ancestors. Louise Bigmeat Maney and her husband, John Henry Maney, produce a highly polished, unglazed earthenware in traditional shapes and patterns. Today they use a potter's wheel, fire in an electric kiln, and purchase clay that is mined locally in North Carolina.

Catawba potter Sara Ayers produced this double chief's head pot by rolling clay into long coils and winding them up layer upon layer.

Cherokee potter Louise Bigmeat Maney created this highly polished black earthenware frog pot from locally mined clay.

218

POTTERY TILES

Like the tradition-bound rural potter, Texan Larry Peña also works with earth materials to make cement tiles by hand, but his workplace is the garage of his small home in San Antonio. Although he acquired respect for the craft from his father, who made tiles in Monterrey, Mexico, he did not learn the skills until moving to Laredo, Texas, in the late 1920s. Larry Peña has been working at his craft since that time.

During his peak years of production in Laredo, he made 360 tiles each day. Today, sixty years later, he starts work in the cool part of the day before sunrise and completes as many as sixty tiles before the heat of the midday sun forces him to stop. He resumes his work at sunrise the next day.

He begins each tile by laying a square, metal pattern

After laying a pattern mold in the bottom of his tile form, Texas tilemaker Larry Peña begins a tile by pouring colored cement into each section of the pattern. He can produce a tile every two minutes.

mold in the bottom of his tile form. With a small scoop, he pours his colors—mixtures of pigment, cement, and water—into different sections of the pattern. When all of the sections have been filled, he takes the pattern mold off, washes it to prevent the buildup of cement, and lays it aside. He then sprinkles dry cement over the wet colors in the form to absorb the excess moisture and pours in unpigmented cement to the top of the form to complete the tile.

While the new tile is still in the form, Mr. Peña applies 150 pounds of pressure to it, pressing out the water, after which he removes the tile and puts it on a rack in the sun to dry. The entire process for each tile takes only two minutes. The next day he soaks the tiles in water and dries them once again, curing them to a strength that will withstand generations of rugged and constant use.

After he lays the tiles, he waxes them with a homemade solution of turpentine, kerosene, and beeswax, buffing them to a lustrous finish that, he says, improves with wear. "The more you dance on them," he quips, "the more they shine!"

The tiles are placed in the sun to dry after Mr. Peña has squeezed out most of the water with the aid of a hydraulic press.

Larry Peña's patio, originally a children's play area, has expanded to a full-sized dance floor.

SELECTED BIBLIOGRAPHY

Basketmaking

Christopher, F. J. *Basketry*. New York: Dover Publications, 1952.

Davis, Gerald L. "Afro-American Coil Basketry in Charleston County, South Carolina." In *American Folklife* by Don Yoder, ed. Austin: University of Texas Press, 1976.

DeWulf, Karol K. "Low-Country Baskets." *Country Home Magazine*, October 1986, pp. 67-73, 122.

Hackley, Larry. *Splits and Splints*. Exhibition Catalog. Atlanta: Southern Arts Federation, 1982.

James, George Wharton. *Practical Basket Making*. Pasadena, CA: George Wharton James, n.d.

Lamb, Frank W. *Indian Baskets of North America*. Riverside, CA: Riverside Museum Press, 1962.

LeBlanc, Jennifer Fortier. *Acadian Palmetto Braiding: The Folk Art of Elvina Kidder*. Exhibition Catalog. Lafayette, LA: Lafayette Natural History Museum Association, 1982.

Leftwick, Rodney L. *Arts and Crafts of the Cherokee*. Glorietta, NM: Rio Grande Press, 1970.

Marshall, Howard Wight. "Mr. Westfall's Baskets: Traditional Craftsmanship in Northcentral Missouri." *Mid-South Folklore* 2 (1974): 43-59.

Myers, Betty. "Gullah Basketry." *Craft Horizons* 36 (June 1976): 30-31, 81.

Rosengarten, Dale. *Row Upon Row: Seagrass Baskets of the South Carolina Lowcountry*. Exhibition Catalog. Columbia: McKissick Museum, University of South Carolina, 1986.

Schiffer, Nancy. *Baskets*. West Chester, PA: Schiffer Publishing, 1984.

Sutherland, David. "Traditional Basketmaking in Kentucky." *Kentucky Folklore Record* 18, no. 4 (1972): 89-92.

Slone, Anthony, prod. *Oaksie*. Film Transcript. Whitesburg, KY: Appalshop, 1980.

Teleki, Gloria Roth. *Collecting Traditional American Basketry*. New York: E. P. Dutton, 1979.

Turnbaugh, Sarah Peabody, and William A. Turnbaugh. *Indian Baskets*. West Chester, PA: Schiffer Publishing, 1986.

Twining, Mary. "Harvesting and Heritage: A Comparison of Afro-American and African Basketry." *Southern Folklore Quarterly* 42 (1978): 159-74.

Toymaking

Barrick, Mac E. "Folk Toys." *Pennsylvania Folklife* 29 (Autumn 1979): 27-34.

Caney, Steven. *Steven Caney's Toy Book*. New York: Workman Publishing Company, 1972.

Comstock, Henry. "Folk Toys Are Back Again." *Popular Science*, March 1960, pp. 144-47.

Culin, Stewart. *Games of the North American Indians*. New York: Dover Publications, 1975.

Fischman, Joshua. "Toys Across Time." *Psychology Today*, October 1985, pp. 56-63.

Fulcher, Robert J. "Rolley Hole Marbles." In *1986 Festival of American Folklife Program*. Festival Program. Washington: Smithsonian Institution, 1986.

Garland, Linda, and Hilton Smith. *The Foxfire Book of Toys and Games*. Rabun Gap, GA: The Foxfire Fund, 1985.

Jailer, Mildred. "Rag and Cloth Dolls." *Hobbies*, March 1985, pp. 34-37.

Lavitt, Wendy. *American Folk Dolls*. New York: Alfred A. Knopf, 1982.

——. "America's Folk Toys." *Clarion*, Winter 1980-81, pp. 42-47.

Mooney, James. "Cherokee Ball Play." *Journal of Cherokee Studies* 7, no. 1 (Spring 1982): 10-24.

Pettit, Florence H. *How to Make Whirligigs and Whimmy Diddles*. New York: Thomas Y. Crowell Company, 1972.

Reed, Mark. "Reflections on Cherokee Stickball." *Journal of Cherokee Studies* 2, no. 1 (Winter 1977): 195-200.

Wynne, Joe. "Rolley Hole!" *Tennessee Conservationist* 52, no. 1 (January-February 1986): 7-9.

Woodworking

Alvey, R. Gerald. *Dulcimer Maker: The Craft of Homer Ledford*. Lexington: University Press of Kentucky, 1984.

Ancelet, Barry Jean. *The Makers of Cajun Music (Musiciens cadiens et creoles)*. In English and French. Austin: University of Texas Press, 1984.

Bristol, Marc. "Dulcimers Revisited." *Mother Earth News*, July-August 1981, pp. 144-45.

Bryan, Charles F. "American Folk Instruments I. The Appalachian Mountain Dulcimer." *Tennessee Folklore Society Bulletin* 18 (March 1952): 1-5.

——. "American Folk Instruments III. Improvised Instruments." *Tennessee Folklore Society Bulletin* 18 (September 1952): 65-67.

Burrell, Melanie, Johnny Ramey, and Fred Sanders. "Using Poplar Bark for Chair Bottoms." *Foxfire* 16, no. 3 (Fall 1982): 210-15.

Comeaux, Malcolm L. "Louisiana Folk Boats." In *1985 Festival of American Folklife Program*. Festival Program. Washington: Smithsonian Institution, 1985.

——. "Origin and Evolution of Mississippi River Fishing Craft." *Pioneer America* 10 (June 1978): 72-97.

Gregory, H. F. "Pirogue Builder: A Vanishing Craftsman." *Louisiana Studies* 3 (Fall 1964): 316-18.

Hastings, S. E., Jr. "Construction Techniques in an Old Appalachian Mountain Dulcimer." *Journal of American Folklore* 83 (October-December 1970): 462-68.

Hodgkinson, Ralph. "Tools of the Woodworker." *History News* 20, no. 5 (May 1965). Technical Leaflet no. 28.

Irwin, John Rice. *Musical Instruments of the Southern Appalachian Mountains*. West Chester, PA: Schiffer Publishing, 1983.

Jones, Michael Owen. " 'For Myself I Likes a 'Decent', Plain-Made Chair': The Concept of Taste and the Traditional Arts in America." *Western Folklore* 31 (January 1972): 27-52.

——. *The Handmade Object and Its Maker*. Berkeley: University of California Press, 1975.

——. " 'If You Make a Simple Thing, You Gotta Sell it at a Simple Price': Folk Art Production as a Business." Parts 1-3. *Kentucky Folklore Record* 17, no. 4 (October-December 1971): 73-77; 18, no. 1 (January-March 1972): 5-12; 18, no. 2 (April-June 1972): 31-40.

Joyner, Charles W. "Dulcimer Making in Western North Carolina: Creativity in a Traditional Mountain Craft." *Southern Folklore Quarterly* 39 (1975): 341-61.

Keller, Michael. "Chairmaking—A Photo Essay." *Goldenseal* 12, no. 3 (Fall 1986): 12-13.

Knipmeyer, William B. "Folk Boats of Eastern French Louisiana." In *American Folklife* by Don Yoder, ed. Austin: University of Texas Press, 1976.

MacLeod, Bruce A. "Quills, Fifes, and Flutes Before the Civil War." *Southern Folklore Quarterly* 42 (1978): 201-208.

Marshall, Howard Wight, and David H. Stanley. "Homemade Boats in South Georgia." *Mississippi Folklore Register* 12 (Fall 1978): 75-94.

Martin, Charles E. " 'Make 'em Fast and Shed 'em Quick': The Appalachian Craftsman Revisited." *Appalachian Journal* 9 (Fall 1981): 4-19.

Milnes, Gerald. "West Virginia Split Bottom." *Goldenseal* 12, no. 3 (Fall 1986): 9-11, 14-15.

Odell, Scott.. "Folk Instruments." *Arts in Virginia* 12 (Fall 1971): 31-37.

Pickow, Peter. *Hammered Dulcimer*. New York: Oak Publications, 1979.

Ritchie, Jean. *Jean Ritchie's Dulcimer People*. New York: Oak Publications, n.d.

Rizzetta, Sam. *Hammer Dulcimer: History and Playing*. Leaflet no. 72-4. Washington: National Museum of American History, 1981.

——. *Making a Hammer Dulcimer*. Leaflet no. 72-5. Washington: National Museum of American History, 1981.

Savoy, Ann Allen. *Cajun Music: A Reflection of A People*. Eunice, LA: Bluebird Press, 1984.

Savoy, Marc. "How to Tune Your Own Cajun Accordion." Photocopy. Eunice, LA: Savoy Music Center, n.d.

Seeger, Charles. "The Appalachian Dulcimer." *Journal of American Folklore* 71 (January-March 1958): 40-51.

Sitton, Thad, and James H. Conrad. *Every Sun That Rises. Wyatt Moore of Caddo Lake*. Austin: University of Texas Press, 1985.

Sloane, Eric. *A Reverence for Wood*. New York: Ballantine Books, 1973.

Street, Julia Montgomery. "Mountain Dulcimer." *North Carolina Folklore* 14 (November 1966): 26-30.

Underhill, Roy. "Chairmaking the Old Time Way." *Mechanix Illustrated*, June 1982, pp. 46-49, 100.

Waldo, Ednard. "The Pirogue." Wildlife Education Bulletin no. 80. Baton Rouge: Louisiana Wild Life and Fisheries Commission, n.d.

Waring, Dennis. *Making Folk Instruments in Wood*. New York: Sterling Publishing Company, 1985.

Sewing

"The Art of Patchwork." *Tennessee Folklore Society Bulletin* 16 (September 1950): 54-61.

Beyer, Jinny. *The Quilter's Album of Blocks and Borders*. McLean, VA: EPM Publications, 1980.

Bishop, Robert. *New Discoveries in American Quilts*. New York: E. P. Dutton, 1975.

Bishop, Robert, William Secord, and Judith Reiter Weissman. *Quilts, Coverlets, Rugs and Samplers*. New York: Alfred A. Knopf, 1982.

Callahan, Nancy. "Helping the Peoples to Help Themselves." *Quilt Digest* 4 (1986): 20-29.

Caulfeild, S. F. A., and Blanche C. Saward. *Encyclopedia of Victorian Needlework*. Vols. 1 and 2. New York: Dover Publications, 1972.

Clarke, Mary Washington. *Kentucky Quilts and Their Makers*. Lexington: University Press of Kentucky, 1976.

Farb, Joanne. "Piecin' and Quiltin': Two Quilters in

Southwest Arkansas." *Southern Folklore Quarterly* 39 (1975): 363-75.

Freeman, Roland L. *Something to Keep You Warm*. Exhibition Catalog. Jackson: Mississippi Department of Archives and History, 1981.

Giganti, Maria, and Carol Clyne. "Ins and Outs of Quilting." *Threads Magazine*, December 1985-January 1986, pp. 64-68.

Hunter Museum of Art. *Quilt Close-up: Five Southern Views*. Exhibition Catalog. Chattanooga, TN: Hunter Museum of Art, 1983.

Ickis, Marguerite. *Standard Book of Quilt Making and Collecting*. New York: Dover Publications, 1949.

Irwin, John Rice. *A People and Their Quilts*. West Chester, PA: Schiffer Publishing, 1984.

Johnson, Bruce. *A Child's Comfort: Baby and Doll Quilts in American Folk Art*. New York: Harcourt Brace Jovanovich, 1977.

Landry, George. "Golden Crown." *Wild Tchoupitoulas*. Stereo Sound Recording ILPS 9360. Los Angeles: Island Records.

——. "Meet De Boys On De Battle Front." *Wild Tchoupitoulas*. Stereo Sound Recording ILPS 9360. Los Angeles: Island Records.

Lee, Andrea. "Quilts (Our Far Flung Correspondents)." *New Yorker*, July 11, 1983, pp. 47-59.

Mellor, Gail McGowan. "Anonymous Had a Name: Kentucky's Legacy of Quilts." *Beaux Arts*, Spring 1982, pp. 22-27.

Meyer, Suellen. "Pine Tree Quilts." *Quilt Digest* 4 (1986): 6-19.

Milspaw, Yvonne. "Appalachian Folk Crafts in Transition." *Goldenseal* 2 (April-June 1976): 14-16, 46-48.

Suter, Betty. "Tatting: Poor Man's Lace That is Really Elegant Finery." *Threads Magazine*, August-September 1986, pp. 64-70.

Torrey, Ella King, and Maude Southwell Wahlman. *Ten Afro-American Quilters*. Exhibition Catalog. Oxford, MS: Center for the Study of Southern Culture, 1983.

Zegart, Shelly. "Old Maid, New Woman." *Quilt Digest* 4 (1986): 54-65.

Woodcarving

Bronner, Simon J. "Folk Techniques of Chain Carving." *Studies in Traditional American Crafts* (1981): 3-19.

——. "Links to Behavior: An Analysis of Chain Carving." *Kentucky Folklore Record* 29, no. 3-4 (July-December 1983): 72-82.

Carpenter, Lisa, and Kevin Sullivan. " 'That Snake Stick Just Took My Eyes'." *Foxfire* 18, no. 3 (Fall 1984): 148-53.

Fleckenstein, Henry A., Jr. *Decoys of the Mid-Atlantic Region*. West Chester, PA: Schiffer Publishing, 1979.

——. *Southern Decoys of Virginia and the Carolinas*. West Chester, PA: Schiffer Publishing, 1983.

Fogelson, Raymond D., and Amelia B. Walker. "Self and Other in Cherokee Booger Masks." *Journal of Cherokee Studies* 5, no. 2 (Fall 1980): 88-102.

Frank, Charles W., Jr. *Wetland Heritage: The Louisiana Duck Decoy*. Gretna, LA: Pelican Publishing Company, 1985.

Grider, Sylvia Ann, and Barbara Ann Allen. "Howard Taylor, Cane Maker and Handle Shaver." *Indiana Folklore* 7, no. 1-2 (1974): 5-25.

Haid, Alan G. *Decoys of the Mississippi Flyway*. West Chester, PA: Schiffer Publishing, 1981.

Havre de Grace Decoy Festival Committee. *Havre de Grace Decoy Festival Program*. Annual Program. Havre de Grace, MD: Havre de Grace Decoy Festival Committee, 1982-86.

Hopkins, C. A. Porter. "Maryland Decoys and Their Makers." *Maryland Conservationist* 42 (November-December 1965): 2-5.

Reuter, Frank. "John Arnold's Link Chains: A Study in Folk Art." *Mid-South Folklore* 5 (Summer 1977): 41-52.

Speck, Frank G., and Leonard Broom. *Cherokee Dance and Drama*. Norman: University of Oklahoma Press, 1983.

U. S. Department of the Interior, Indian Arts and Crafts Board. *Allen Long: Cherokee Mask Maker*. Exhibition Catalog. Washington: U.S. Department of the Interior, 1975.

Broommaking

Archbold, Annelen. "Percy Beeson, A Kentucky Broommaker." *Mid-South Folkore* 3 (Summer 1975): 41-45.

Best, Martha S. "The Art of Making Brooms." *Pennsylvania Folklife Festival Supplement* 26 (July 1977): 40-41.

Lornell, Christopher. "Coy Thompson, Afro-American Corn Shuck Mop Maker: 'We Make Them Now to Show the Younger People How the Older Ones Come Up.' " *Tennessee Folklore Society Bulletin* 42 (December 1976): 175-80.

Spinning, Dyeing & Weaving

Adrosko, Rita J. *Natural Dyes and Home Dyeing*. New York: Dover Publications, 1971.

Atwater, Mary Meigs. *The Shuttle-Craft Book of American Hand-Weaving*. New York: Macmillan Company, 1971.

Bulbach, Stanley. "Why Bother With Natural Dyeing?" *Threads Magazine*, June-July 1986, pp. 32-37.

Erickson, Johanna. "Rag Rugs: Not Always Made From Rags." *Threads Magazine*, February-March 1986, pp. 40-41.

Florentine, Gemma. "Spindle and Distaff." *Threads Magazine*, December 1985-January 1986, pp. 33-35.

Franklin, Sue. "My Affair With King Cotton." *Threads Magazine*, February-March 1987, p. 39.

Johnson, Geraldine Niva. *Weaving Rag Rugs: A Women's Craft in Western Maryland*. Knoxville: University of Tennessee Press, 1985.

Krechniak, Helen Bullard. "Vegetable Dyeing Revival in the Southern Appalachians." *Tennessee Folklore Society Bulletin* 27 (September 1961): 48-51.

Louisiana State Museum. *L'Amour de Maman: La tradition acadienne du tissage en Louisiane*. Exhibition Catalog. New Orleans: Louisiana State Museum, 1983.

Messenger, Betty. *Picking Up the Linen Threads*. Austin: University of Texas Press, 1975.

Post, Lauren C. "The Cotton and Corn Country." In *Cajun Sketches: From the Prairies of Southwest Louisiana*. Baton Rouge: Louisiana State University Press, 1962.

Stone, Helen Wilmer. "Vegetable Dyes." *Mountain Life and Work*, April 1930, pp. 31-32.

Svinicki, Eunice. *Step By Step Spinning and Dyeing*. Racine, WI: Western Publishing Company, 1974.

Thornburgh, Kathleen. "Colors From Nature." *Tennessee Conservationist* 40, no. 7 (July 1974): 14-15.

Ward, Sophia. "Acadian Spinning, Dyeing, and Weaving." *Louisiana Folklife* 3, no. 2 (October 1978): 19-34.

Ware, J. O., and L. I. Benedict. "Colored Cottons and Their Economic Value." *Journal of Heredity* 53, no. 2 (March-April 1962): 57-65.

Wilson, Sadye Tune, and Doris Finch Kennedy. *Of Coverlets: The Legacies, The Weavers*. Nashville: Tunstede, 1983.

Metalworking & Leather Tooling

Boatright, Mody C. "How Will Boatright Made Bits and Spurs." *Journal of American Folklore* 83 (January-March 1970): 77-80.

Council for Small Industries in Rural Areas. *Catalogue of Drawings for Wrought Ironwork*. England: Council for Small Industries in Rural Areas, 1973.

Johnson, Evert A. "Black Metal." *American Craft* 43, no. 4 (August-September 1983): 11-15, 80.

Kauffman, Henry J. *Early American Ironware*. New York: Weathervane Books, 1966.

Keller, Michael. "Between Hammer and Anvil." *Goldenseal* 12, no. 1 (Spring 1986): 9-15.

Meilach, Dona Z. *Decorative and Sculptural Ironwork*. New York: Crown Publishers, 1977.

Puckett, Jim, and Bob Smith. *Mississippi Blacksmithing*. Exhibition Catalog. Laurel, MS: Lauren Rogers Museum of Art, 1986.

Schmirler, Otto. *Werk und Werkzug des Kunstschmieds*. Austria: Verlag Ernst Wasmuth Fubingen, 1981.

——. *Wrought Iron Artistry*. Lompoc, CA: Larson Publishing Company, n.d.

Streeter, Donald. *Professional Smithing*. New York: Charles Scribner's Sons, 1980.

Vlach, John Michael. *Charleston Blacksmith: The Work of Phillip Simmons*. Athens: University of Georgia Press, 1981.

——. "The Craftsman and the Communal Image, Phillip Simmons: Charleston Blacksmith." *Family Heritage* 2 (February 1979): 14-19.

——. "The Fabrication of a Traditional Fire Tool." *Journal of American Folklore* 86, no. 339 (January 1973): 54-56.

——. "Phillip Simmons: Afro-American Blacksmith." In *Black People and Their Culture: Selected Writings From the African Diaspora* by Rosie L. Hooks, et al. Washington: Smithsonian Institution Press, 1976.

Potterymaking

Auman, Dorothy Cole, and Charles Zug III. "Nine Generations of Potters: The Cole Family." *Southern Exposure* 5 (Summer-Fall 1977): 166-74.

Burrell, Melanie, Lynne Kilby, and Patsy Singleton. "Cleater Meaders Builds a Kiln." *Foxfire* 17, no. 3 (Fall 1983): 147-65.

Burrison, John A. "Afro-American Folk Pottery in the South." *Southern Folklore Quarterly* 42 (1978): 175-99.

——. "Alkaline-Glazed Stoneware: A Deep South Pottery Tradition." *Southern Folklore Quarterly* 39 (1975): 377-403.

——. *Brothers in Clay: The Story of Georgia Folk Pottery*. Athens: University of Georgia Press, 1983.

——. "Clay Clans: Georgia's Pottery Dynasties." *Family Heritage* 2 (June 1979): 70-77.

Coyne, John. "A Dynasty of Folk Potters." *Americana*, March-April 1980, pp. 40-45.

Fields, Mary Durland. "Jugtown Pottery." *Ceramics Monthly* 31 (March 1983): 53-60.

Greer, Georgeanna H. "Alkaline Glazes and Groundhog Kilns: Southern Pottery Traditions." *Antiques*, April 1977, pp. 768-73.

——. "Groundhog Kilns—Rectangular American

Kilns of the Nineteenth and Early Twentieth Centuries." *Northeast Historical Archaeology* 6 (1977): 42-54.

Myers, Susan H. "A Survey of Traditional Pottery Manufacture in the Mid-Atlantic and Northeastern United States." *Northeast Historical Archaeology* 6 (1977): 1-13.

North Carolina Museum of Art. *Jugtown Pottery: The Busbee Vision*. Exhibition Catalog. Raleigh: North Carolina Museum of Art, 1984.

Rinzler, Ralph, and Robert Sayers. *The Meaders Family: North Georgia Potters*. Smithsonian Folklife Studies, no. 1. Washington: Smithsonian Institution Press, 1980.

Sanders, Fred, and Milton Brock. "Lanier Meaders: Folk Potter." *Foxfire* 16, no. 1 (Spring 1982): 3-16.

Scarborough, Quincy J., Jr. *North Carolina Decorated Stoneware: The Webster School of Folk Potters*. Fayetteville, NC: Scarborough Press, 1986.

Sweezy, Nancy. *Raised in Clay: The Southern Pottery Tradition*. Washington: Smithsonian Institution Press, 1984.

Wigginton, Eliot, and Margie Bennett, eds. *Foxfire 8*. New York: Doubleday, Anchor Press, 1984.

Zug, Charles G., III. "Jugtown Reborn: The North Carolina Folk Potter in Transition." *Pioneer America Society Transactions* 3 (1980): 1-23.

——. *Turners and Burners: The Folk Potters of North Carolina*. Chapel Hill: University of North Carolina Press, 1986.

General Background Reading

Abnernethy, Francis Edward, ed. *Folk Art in Texas*. Dallas: Southern Methodist University Press and Texas Folklore Society, 1985.

Alexandria Museum/Visual Art Center. *Doing it Right and Passing it On: North Louisiana Folk Crafts*. Exhibition Catalog. Alexandria, VA: Alexandria Museum/Visual Art Center, 1981.

Andrews, Edward D. *The Community Industries of the Shakers*. New York: University of the State of New York, 1933. Reprint. Charlestown, MA: Emporium Publications, 1971.

Atlanta Historical Society. *Tangible Traditions: Folk Crafts of Georgia and Neighboring States*. Exhibition Catalog. Atlanta: Atlanta Historical Society, 1984.

Ben-Amos, Dan. "Toward a Definition of Folklore in Context." *Journal of American Folklore* 84, no. 331 (January-March 1971): 3-15.

Bronner, Simon J., ed. *American Material Culture and Folklife: A Prologue and Dialogue*. Ann Arbor: UMI Research Press, 1985.

Bulger, Peggy A. "Defining Folk Arts for the Working Folklorist." *Kentucky Folklore Record* 26, no.

1-2 (January-June 1980): 62-66.

Bullard, Helen. *Crafts and Craftsmen of the Tennessee Mountains.* Falls Church, VA: The Summit Press, 1976.

Camp, Charles, ed. and comp. *Traditional Craftsmanship in America: A Diagnostic Report.* Washington: National Council for the Traditional Arts, 1983.

Chase, Judith Wragg. "American Heritage from Antebellum Black Craftsmen." *Southern Folklore Quarterly* 42 (1978): 135-58.

Coe, Ralph T. *Lost and Found Traditions: Native American Art 1965-1985.* New York: American Federation of Arts, 1986.

Comeaux, Malcolm L. *Atchafalaya Swamp Life: Settlement and Folk Occupations.* Geoscience and Man, vol. 2. Baton Rouge: School of Geoscience, Louisiana State University, 1972.

Comstock, Helen. "Chronology of Crafts." *Antiques,* October 1959, pp. 324-27.

Creekmore, Betsey B. *Traditional American Crafts.* New York: Hearthside Press, 1968.

deCaro, F. A., and R. A. Jordan. *Louisiana Traditional Crafts.* Baton Rouge: Louisiana State University, 1980.

Dorson, Richard M., ed. *Folklore and Folklife: An Introduction.* Chicago: University of Chicago Press, 1972.

Durrance, Jill, and William Shamblin, eds. *Appalachian Ways.* Washington: Appalachian Regional Commission, 1976.

Dyal, Susan. *Preserving Traditional Arts.* Los Angeles: American Indian Studies Center, UCLA, 1985.

Earnest, Adele. *Folk Art in America: A Personal View.* West Chester, PA: Schiffer Publishing, 1984.

Eaton, Allen H. *Handicrafts of the Southern Highlands.* New York: Dover Publications, 1973.

Feder, Norman. *American Indian Art.* New York: Harrison House/Harry N. Abrams, 1982.

Ferris, William. *Afro-American Folk Art and Crafts.* Boston: G. K. Hall, 1983.

———. "Black Folk Art and Crafts: A Mississippi Sample." Photo Essay. *Southern Folklore Quarterly* 42 (1978): 209-41.

———. *Local Color: A Sense of Place in Folk Art.* New York: McGraw-Hill Book Company, 1982.

Fontenot, Mary Alice, and Julie Landry. *The Louisiana Experience: An Introduction to the Culture of the Bayou State.* Baton Rouge: Claitor's Publishing Division, 1983.

Foreman, Grant. *The Five Civilized Tribes.* Norman: University of Oklahoma Press, 1934.

Georgia Writer's Program. *Drums and Shadows.* Garden City, NY: Doubleday, Anchor Press, 1972.

Guirard, Greg. *Seasons of Light in the Atchafalaya Basin.* St. Martinville, LA: Catahoula Cypress and Photograph Co., 1983.

Jasper, Pat, and Kay Turner. *Art Among Us.* Exhibition Catalog. San Antonio: San Antonio Museum Association, 1986.

Joyner, Charles W. *Down By the Riverside: A South Carolina Slave Community.* Urbana: University of Illinois Press, 1984.

King, Duane H. *Cherokee Heritage: Official Guidebook to the Museum of the Cherokee Indian.* Cherokee, NC: Museum of the Cherokee Indian, 1984.

Lucie-Smith, Edward. *The Story of Craft: The Craftsman's Role in Society.* New York: Van Nostrand Reinhold Company, 1984.

Mississippi Department of Archives and History. *Made By Hand: Mississippi Folk Art.* Exhibition Catalog. Jackson: Mississippi Department of Archives and History, 1980.

Moore, J. Roderick. "Folk Crafts." *Arts in Virginia* 12 (Fall 1971): 23-29.

Mull, J. Alexander, and Gordon Boger. *Recollections of the Catawba Valley.* Boone, NC: Appalachian Consortium Press, 1983.

Peek, Phil. "Afro-American Material Culture and the Afro-American Craftsman." *Southern Folklore Quarterly* 42 (1978): 109-34.

Sayers, Robert. "Traditional Southern Crafts in the Twentieth Century." In *1981 Festival of American Folklife Program.* Festival Program. Washington: Smithsonian Institution, 1981, 17-19.

Seymour, John. *The Forgotten Crafts.* New York: Alfred A. Knopf, 1984.

Smith, Michael P. *Spirit World: Pattern in the Expressive Folk Culture of Afro-American New Orleans.* Exhibition Catalog. New Orleans: New Orleans Urban Folklife Society, 1984.

Spitzer, Nicholas R. *Louisiana Folklife: A Guide to the State.* Baton Rouge: Louisiana Folklife Program/Division of the Arts, 1985.

Sprigg, June. *Shaker Design.* Exhibition Catalog. New York: Whitney Museum of American Art, 1986.

Steinfeldt, Cecilia. *Texas Folk Art: One Hundred Fifty Years of the Southwestern Tradition.* Austin: Texas Monthly Press, 1981.

Terry, George D., and Lynn Robertson Myers, eds. *Carolina Folk: The Cradle of a Southern Tradition.* Exhibition Catalog. Columbia: McKissick Museum, University of South Carolina, 1985.

Thompson, Robert Farris. *Flash of the Spirit: African and Afro-American Art and Philosophy.* New York: Random House, Vintage Books, 1984.

Tuan, Yi-Fu. "The Significance of the Artifact." *Journal of American Folklore* 83 (October-December 1970): 462-72.

Twain, Mark. *Life on the Mississippi.* New York: New American Library, 1961.

Vlach, John Michael. *The Afro-American Tradition in Decorative Arts.* Exhibition Catalog. Cleveland: Cleveland Museum of Fine Art, 1978.

Wadsworth, Anna. *Missing Pieces: Georgia Folk Art, 1770-1976.* Exhibition Catalog. Tucker: Georgia Council for the Arts and Humanities, 1976.

Ward, Dan. "Condensed Introduction to the Craftperson's Work and Tradition." *Studies in Traditional American Crafts* (1979): 5-19.

Whisnant, David E. *All That is Native and Fine: The Politics of Culture in an American Region.* Chapel Hill: University of North Carolina Press, 1983.

———. *Modernizing the Mountaineer: People, Power, and Planning in Appalachia.* Boone, NC: Appalachian Consortium Press, 1980.

Wigginton, Eliot, ed. *Foxfire 3.* Garden City, NY: Doubleday, Anchor Press, 1975.

———. *Foxfire 4.* Garden City, NY: Doubleday, Anchor Press, 1977.

———. *Foxfire 5.* Garden City, NY: Doubleday, Anchor Press, 1979.

———. *Foxfire 6.* Garden City, NY: Doubleday, Anchor Press, 1980.

Wolfe, Charles K. *Tennessee Strings: The Story of Country Music in Tennessee.* Knoxville: The University of Tennessee Press, 1977.

Wraga, William C. "Craftsmanship and Creativity in Modern Society." *New Jersey Folklore* 2 (Spring 1977): 8-15.

Yoder, Don, ed. *American Folklife.* Austin: University of Texas Press, 1976.

RESOURCES

Workshops

The following schools and organizations sponsor workshops in a variety of traditional crafts, which range from a single day to several weeks in length. All of them offer a free brochure or booklet describing their programs, and those that require a self-addressed, stamped envelope (SASE) are noted. A dagger (†) indicates that the building is accessible to the handicapped; two daggers (††) indicate that the building is partially accessible to the handicapped.

Appalachian Center for Crafts
Tennessee Technological University
Route 3, Box 347 A-1
Smithville, TN 38505
(615) 597-6801
One-week summer workshops in art, design and traditional crafts are offered at a campus of nearly 600 acres overlooking Center Hill Lake in Middle Tennessee. †

Arrowmont School of Arts and Crafts
P.O. Box 567, Gatlinburg, TN 37738
(615) 436-5860
Workshops range from one week to two weeks in beginner, intermediate and advanced levels of various traditional and contemporary arts and crafts on a 70-acre visual-arts complex. †

Augusta Heritage Arts Workshop
Davis and Elkins College
Elkins, WV 26241
(304) 636-1903
More than 85 summer classes ranging from one weekend to three weeks present various aspects of traditional crafts and folklore. †

Columbia Art and Folk Center
P.O. Box 682, Columbia, LA 71418
(318) 649-6722
One-day to one-week workshops are offered on a wide variety of traditional crafts. †

Hambidge Center for Creative Arts and Sciences
P.O. Box 339, Rabun Gap, GA 30568
(404) 746-5718
Day-long to week-long workshops and two-week to two-month-long residencies are held on 600 acres of serene woodlands in northeast Georgia. Send SASE for information and applications. †

John C. Campbell Folk School
Route 1, Brasstown, NC 28902
(704) 837-2775
Classes in Appalachian and contemporary crafts, folk music, and dance, from beginner to advanced levels, are offered in a beautiful mountain setting. Annual calendar available for more information. †

Montgomery Technical College
Continuing Education Department
P.O. Box 787, Troy, NC 27371
(919) 572-3691
Summer workshops and short classes in traditional craft techniques are offered at this school in south central North Carolina. †

Oscar Farris Tennessee Agricultural Museum
Ellington Agricultural Center
P.O. Box 40627, Nashville, TN 37204
(615) 360-0197
Traditional crafts workshops and demonstrations are offered for different age groups at this restored farm museum. †

Ozark Folk Center
P.O. Box 500, Mountain View, AR 72560
(501) 269-3851
Workshops and demonstrations of crafts from 1820–1920 are offered in season at this Arkansas state park. †

Ozark Regional Crafts Association
P.O. Box 800, Mountain View, AR 72560
A wide selection of training programs and workshops are offered by this crafts association. †

Penland School
Penland, NC 28765
(704) 765-2359
Workshops ranging from one week to eight weeks are offered on Penland's 400-acre campus. ††

Southern Highland Handicraft Guild
P.O. Box 9545, Asheville, NC 28815
(704) 298-7928
A variety of workshops ranging from one day to a week are offered at the guild's Folk Art Center for several levels of ability. †

Clubs & Organizations

The following clubs and organizations, open for membership to the general public, promote interest in the preservation of regional folkways. Many of them publish newsletters or journals containing articles of topical interest, and some sponsor festivals or other activities promoting traditional culture. All have membership levels starting at $15 or less.

American Folklore Society
1703 New Hampshire Avenue, NW
Washington, DC 20009
The American Folklore Society, through its two journals, *Journal of American Folklore* (quarterly) and *American Folklore Society Newsletter* (bimonthly), presents scholarly research into the field of folklore and gives current information about grants, programs, and other issues and events of current interest. The society publishes books, journals, and newsletters and holds annual meetings.

Atlanta Historical Society
3101 Andrews Drive, NW
Atlanta, GA 30305
The Atlanta Historical Society supports the preservation of Atlanta's cultural history. It publishes a bimonthly *Newsletter* and the quarterly *Atlanta Historical Journal*. It also maintains the McElreath Galleries, the Swan and Tullie Smith Houses, a library/archive, and the Philip Trammell Shutze collection. Members enjoy speakers, films, concerts, seminars, and travel opportunities.

Delaware Folklife Project
2 Crestwood Place
Wilmington, DE 19809
The Delaware Folklife Project seeks to document and present the traditional cultures of the state of Delaware. Members receive a quarterly newsletter, *Folklife News*, and can participate in festivals, lectures, exhibitions, audiovisual programs, and meetings.

Florida Folklore Society
P.O. Box 265, White Springs, FL 32096

The Florida Folklore Society, which is affiliated with the Bureau of Florida Folklife, publishes the *Florida Folklore Society Newsletter* and seeks to encourage individuals to recognize and appreciate folklore and folklife in the state. The society sponsors workshops, meetings, and seminars and participates in a number of festivals in the state.

Folklife Society of Louisiana
Northwestern State University
Box 3663, Natchitoches, LA 71497
The Folklife Society of Louisiana is an agency of the Louisiana Folklife Center, which promotes folklife research. *Louisiana Folklife Magazine*, published annually, features articles on crafts, legends, and other topics of interest to folklife researchers and lay people. The society also sponsors an annual conference and cooperates with various organizations to sponsor the Natchitoches-Northwestern Folk Festival.

Folklore Society of Greater Washington
P.O. Box 19114
20th Street Station
Washington, DC 20036
The Folklore Society of Greater Washington is an organization dedicated to preserving and promoting the many forms of folklore in the District of Columbia area. It sponsors monthly programs, weekly dances, workshops, and several annual festivals. Members receive the *Newsletter* monthly, as well as free admission to many of the society's functions.

Missouri Folklore Society
P.O. Box 1757, Columbia, MO 65205
The Missouri Folklore Society encourages the collection, preservation, and study of folklore throughout the state of Missouri. The *Newsletter*, published three times a year, and the *Missouri Folklore Society Journal*, published annually, come with membership. Annual meetings include displays of folk arts and crafts, publications, topical papers, and other events in keeping with the society.

North Carolina Folklore Society
Department of English

RESOURCES

Appalachian State University
Boone, NC 28608
The North Carolina Folklore Society encourages and supports the appreciation and study of North Carolina folklife. Its semiannual *North Carolina Folklore Journal* publishes studies of North Carolina folklore and folklife. The quarterly *Newsletter of the North Carolina Folklore Society* includes news, reviews, and a folklife calendar, all to promote an information network among society members. Both publications come with society membership.

Ozark States Folklore Society
Arkansas College, Batesville, AR 72501
The Ozark States Folklore Society promotes folklore research in the central United States by publishing scholarly articles of general interest in their semiannual *Mid-America Folklore* and sponsors an annual meeting in conjunction with other societies.

Shenandoah Valley Folklore Society
326 Broadway Avenue
Broadway, VA 22815
The Shenandoah Valley Folklore Society emphasizes the regional customs, arts, crafts, music, and everyday life of the Shenandoah Valley. It holds several meetings of topical interest throughout the year and publishes a newsletter, which comes with the membership.

Tennessee Folklore Society
Middle Tennessee State University
Box 201, Murfreesboro, TN 37132
The Tennessee Folklore Society studies the folklore and traditional culture of Tennessee and the mid-South. The society publishes the quarterly *Tennessee Folklore Society Bulletin*, as well as other folklore-related works. An annual meeting held in the fall presents entertaining programs of interest to scholars and lay persons alike. A record series documents traditional mid-South music and spoken word; each record includes a substantial booklet of annotations.

Texas Folklore Society
P.O. Box 13007, SFA Station
Nacogdoches, TX 75962
The Texas Folklore Society stimulates the recording and study of the folk culture of Texas and the Southwest. It publishes an annual volume of folklore research or of topical folklore interest and a biannual newsletter of society happenings.

Virginia Folklore Society
115 Wilson Hall, University of Virginia
Charlottesville, VA 22903
The Virginia Folklore Society collects and studies the folk culture of Virginia. It publishes a journal, *Folklore and Folklife in Virginia*, on an irregular basis and also sponsors an annual meeting.

Libraries, Archives, & Folklife Centers

The institutions listed below have information on traditional crafts in a variety of formats, including slides, photographs, books, papers, and audio- and videotapes. In many cases these institutions have small staffs and may not be open to walk-in traffic. Advance notice of your topic of interest and a request for an appointment time is usually required, either in writing or by telephone. A dagger (†) indicates that the building is accessible to the handicapped; two daggers (††) indicate that the building is partially accessible to the handicapped.

Abby Aldrich Rockefeller Folk Art Center
Colonial Williamsburg Foundation
P.O. Box C, Williamsburg, VA 23187
(804) 229-1000 ext. 2424
The center has an extensive library and permanent folk art collection in its museum. ††

American Craft Council Library
45 West 45th Street, New York, NY 10036
(212) 869-9462
This library contains an artists' registry and archives, books, catalogs and periodicals, as well as clipping files, a slide collection, and newsletters of craft organizations. †

Appalachian Oral History Project
Alice Lloyd College—Project Director
Pippa Passes, KY 41844
(606) 368-2101 ext. 250
also at:
Lee's Junior College
Jackson, KY 41339
(606) 666-7521
and
Emory and Henry College
Emory, VA 24327
(703) 944-3121
and
Appalachian State University
202 Appalachian Street
Boone, NC 28607
(704) 262-2095
The Appalachian Oral History Project, in

a four-school consortium, has taped approximately 5,000 hours of interviews with residents of the central Appalachian region. Many of the interviews have been transcribed and the collection is catalogued. †

Archive of Folk Culture
Library of Congress
10 First Street SE, Washington, DC 20540
(202) 287-5510
The archive publishes a series of free reference and finding aids, available upon request, which are designed to assist researchers in the fields of folk culture, folklife, and ethnomusicology. †

Archives of Appalachia
East Tennessee State University
Sherrod Library
Box 22450A, Johnson City, TN 37614
(615) 929-4338
The archive serves as a repository that helps document the political, social, cultural, historical and economic development of south central Appalachia. Its holdings include personal and institutional records, vertical files of clippings, Appalachian publications files, audio- and videotapes, and photographs. †

Arkansas State University Folklore Archive
English Department
Arkansas State University
Jonesboro, AR 72401
(501) 972-3043
This archive consists primarily of student-collected manuscripts and tapes, with some works on folk crafts. The collection is partially indexed. †

Barker Texas History Center
University of Texas
Sid Richardson Hall 2.101
Austin, TX 78713
(512) 471-5961
The center's collection, which dates back to 1883, has extensive historical material on Texas and the South. †

Blue Ridge Heritage Archive,
Ferrum College
Blue Ridge Institute
Ferrum, VA 24088
(703) 365-2121 ext. 416
The archive houses a large collection of materials documenting the folklife and history of Virginia. Subjects include traditional music, crafts, architecture, story-

telling, foodways, and agricultural techniques. †

Center for Southern Folklore
1216 Peabody Avenue
P.O. Box 40105, Memphis, TN 38174
(901) 726-4205
The center maintains a multimedia folk culture archive of historical and contemporary film footage, slides, recordings, and photographs. It also sells and rents films, videos, and exhibits on Southern folk art, music, and storytelling. A professional folklore and media staff is available to assist in research. †

Doris Ulmann Galleries
Berea College
C.P.O. 2342, Berea, KY 40404
(606) 986-9341 ext. 5530
The Doris Ulmann Collection is composed of approximately 3,000 photos of Appalachia taken by Doris Ulmann in the late 1920s and early 1930s, including many of area craftspeople. Several are reproduced in this book. †

Florida Folklife Archive
P.O. Box 265, White Springs, FL 32096
(904) 397-2192
The archive contains extensive materials on many ethnic groups, as well as documentation of Florida folklife. It also houses research collections of other folklorists, including tapes, films, and slides. †

Fort New Salem
Salem College, Salem, WV 26426
(304) 782-5245
This archive houses a large collection of craft and museum library resources on furniture, tools, clothing, and fibers, with an emphasis on the period from 1790 to 1830. †

Historic New Orleans Collection
533 Royal Street, New Orleans, LA 70130
(504) 523-4662
The collection houses a research center with three branches: library, manuscripts, and curatorial divisions. Their materials relate to the history and culture of Louisiana and the colonial Gulf Coast. †

Hunter Library Special Collections
Western Carolina University
Cullowhee, NC 28723
(704) 227-7474
This library has several collections of materials on folklife and lore, in addition to

materials about the Cherokee Indians. †

Hutchins Library, Special Collections
Berea College
Berea, KY 40404
(606) 986-9341 ext. 5262
This library houses the Weatherford-Hammond Mountain Collection, the Southern Appalachian Archives, an Appalachian vertical file, and an archive of crafts-related materials. †

Indiana University Folklore Archives
Folklore Institute, Indiana University
103 Morrison Hall
Bloomington, IN 47405
(812) 335-3652
Collections of folklore materials relating to crafts, material culture, tools, and more are housed in this extensive archive. In addition, some collections have photos, slides and cassette tapes of interviews.

Kentucky Library and Museum
Folklife Archives, Kentucky Building
Western Kentucky University
Bowling Green, KY 42101
(502) 745-2592 (library);
745-6086 (folklife archives)
This collection has tapes, student and faculty research, and photos pertaining to folklore and traditional music in Kentucky and the surrounding region. †

Kentucky Department for Libraries and Archives
300 Coffee Tree Road
Frankfort, KY 40602
(502) 875-7000
This institution contains information on folklore in the Kentuckiana and Lincoln Trail Regions. Records are housed both in the state archives at the above address or at each county public library in the two regions. †

Louisiana Folklife Center
Northwestern State University
Box 3663, Natchitoches, LA 71497
(318) 357-4332
This center houses a collection of more than 400 live performance folklife recordings, an extensive group of photographs, and a small library. There is some crafts documentation and Southern studies material. †

Missouri Cultural Heritage Center
University of Missouri
Conley House

Conley & Sanford Streets
Columbia, MO 65211
(314) 882-6296
The center has video, audio, and photographic documentation of traditional arts and folklife throughout Missouri. There are also exhibits and projects dealing with Missouri history, culture, and folklife. †

Mountain Heritage Center
Western Carolina University
Cullowhee, NC 28723
(704) 227-7129
The center's collection contains artifacts representing Southern Appalachian life from prehistoric times to the twentieth century. †

Northern Virginia Folklife Center
George Mason University
4400 University Drive, Fairfax, VA 22030
(703) 323-2221
This collection has materials on textiles (quilting, lacemaking, knitting), with the primary emphasis on family and suburban folklore. Mostly student collected. †

Ozark Folk Center
P.O. Box 500, Mountain View, AR 72560
(501) 269-3851
The library at the center houses resource materials on the region's folklore and traditions. †

Pensacola Historical Museum Library
405 South Adams Street
Pensacola, FL 32501
(904) 433-1559
This library houses historical materials on Pensacola and northwest Florida. †

Smithsonian Folklife Program Archives
Smithsonian Institution
955 L'Enfant Plaza, Suite 2600
Washington, DC 20560
(202) 287-3424
The archive houses oral folklore and items relating to the annual Festival of American Folklife. †

South Carolina Historical Society Archive
Fireproof Building, Charleston, SC 29401
(803) 723-3225
The archive has materials on low country basketmaking and Edgefield pottery, in addition to a large manuscript collection on South Carolina history.

Southern Highland Handicraft Guild Library

Folk Art Center
P.O. Box 9545, Asheville, NC 28815
(704) 298-7928
The library at the center has books, periodicals, and slides that document the craft traditions, folklore, and folklife of the area. †

Southern Historical Collection
Wilson Library
University of North Carolina
Chapel Hill, NC 27514
(919) 962-1345
The collection is a major repository of manuscripts, many of value to folklore research. The collection includes the papers of John C. and Olive Dame Campbell (founders of the John C. Campbell Folk School), the Penn School, the UNC Southern Oral History program, and more. Also present on the UNC campus are the holdings of the Ackland Art Museum, including pottery, paintings, and sculpture by traditional and naive artists of North Carolina and the South. †

Special Collections Library
University of Tennessee Library
Cumberland Avenue
Knoxville, TN 37996
(615) 974-4480
This library houses the Norbert F. Riedl collection of Southern Appalachian folk culture and materials from student folklore projects. †

Tennessee State Parks Folklife Project
403 7th Avenue North
Nashville, TN 37219
(615) 741-2764
The Folklife Project contains the notes, recordings, and photos of folklorists working for the Department of Conservation through the state parks. The emphasis is on local residents who practice folk traditions. †

Traditional Craft Archive
Madison County Historical Society
435 Main Street, Oneida, NY 13421
(315) 363-4136
The archive consists of 10,000 slides, 40 tapes, and 39 films documenting traditional American crafts.

University of Mississippi Blues Archive
Farley Hall, University of Mississippi
University, MS 38677
(601) 232-7753

The Blues Archive, a branch of the John Davis Williams Library, houses the Kenneth S. Goldstein Folklore Collection. This collection consists of books, periodicals, and phonograph records covering all aspects of folklore, with a strong emphasis on Southern folklore. †

University of Texas Institute of Texan Cultures
801 South Bowie Street
P.O. Box 1226, San Antonio, TX 78294
(512) 226-7651
The library at the institute contains books, periodicals, vertical files, audiovisual materials, and a large collection of historical photos. The emphasis is on Texas history and folklore and the ethnic groups that settled the state. †

W.L. Eury Appalachian Collection
Appalachian State University
Boone, NC 28608
(704) 262-4041
The collection contains materials relating to the Southern Appalachian region. Local history, folk music, folklore, and the folk arts are all represented for the approximately 200 counties that comprise the region. In addition, there are microform, audio, and video resources available. †

Winterthur Libraries
Route 52, Winterthur, DE 19735
(302) 656-8591
The manuscript collection at Winterthur has extensive holdings on American craftsmen and their work from the seventeenth to the nineteenth centuries. It houses primary manuscript sources, secondary sources, periodicals, and photographs relating to decorative arts and material culture made or used in colonial America to the end of World War I. It also houses printed sources and periodicals providing broad cultural, economic, and social history context for American decorative arts and material culture. Subjects can be searched by craft or by artist name. †

State Folklore Programs
The following programs within each state serve the public by documenting their regions' folklife resources and activities and offering a variety of public programs to disseminate this information.

Alabama State Council on the Arts and Humanities
One Dexter Avenue
Montgomery, AL 36130
The Alabama Folklife Program within this state agency helps preserve traditional Alabama folk culture and also documents Alabama's folklife resources. Grants for documentation, festivals, surveys, and performances, as well as technical assistance grants for folklife programming, are available.

Arkansas Arts Council
The Heritage Center, Suite 200
225 East Markham
Little Rock, AR 72201
The Arkansas Folk Arts Program serves to promote an awareness and an appreciation of the state's traditional culture and heritage. The Arts Council provides support for a variety of folk arts activities, including performances, exhibitions and tours, documentation projects, films and recordings, workshops, festivals, publications, and apprenticeships. Other activities include a survey of traditional craftspeople, technical assistance for artists, a folklore curriculum, folk arts internships, and the publication of a newsletter.

Bureau of Florida Folklife Programs
P.O. Box 265, White Springs, FL 32096
The Bureau of Florida Folklife Programs is charged with documenting and presenting the folk arts, folklore, and folklife of Florida. It coordinates the Florida Folk Festival; manages the Florida Folklife Archive; conducts Folklife in Education projects in schools; produces slide/tape, radio, and videotape programs, record albums, and traveling exhibits; presents workshops, seminars, and conferences; and provides a variety of technical assistance.

Folk Arts Program
Kentucky Center for the Arts
5 Riverfront Plaza, Louisville, KY 40202
The Folk Arts Program at the Kentucky Center for the Arts covers research and presentation of the folk arts. Areas of emphasis include field research, documentation, exhibition, and presentation via concerts and workshops.

Georgia Endowment for the Humanities
Emory University
1589 Clifton Road, NE

Atlanta, GA 30322
The Georgia Endowment for the Humanities employs a Folklife Program director who coordinates folklife programming in Georgia, conducts field research throughout the state, and fosters community-based folklife research and programs. In addition, it sponsors the Georgia Humanities Resource Center, which documents and presents folklife through videotapes and exhibits. Grants are available from the endowment for projects involving folklife documentation, research, interpretation, and presentation.

Louisiana Crafts Program
Division of the Arts
P.O. Box 44247, Baton Rouge, LA 70804
The Louisiana Crafts Program assists Louisiana craftspeople in marketing and promoting their works. This assistance comes in the form of a directory of master traditional and contemporary craftsmen, marketing workshops, an annual crafts market, and a newsletter. The program works in conjunction with the Louisiana Folklife Program (see below).

Louisiana Folklife Program
Division of the Arts
P.O. Box 44247, Baton Rouge, LA 70804
The Louisiana Folklife Program identifies, documents, preserves, and presents the folk cultural resources of Louisiana. It awards grants to artists and organizations for folklife activities. The program assists in the production of films, videotapes, radio programs, field recordings, records, and photographs for exhibition and distribution purposes throughout the state.

Maryland State Arts Council
15 West Mulberry Street
Baltimore, MD 21201
The Maryland State Arts Council is the state granting agency for the arts. Its folklife program supports documentation and presentation of traditional arts.

Mississippi Department of Archives and History
Mississippi Arts Commission
P.O. Box 571, Jackson, MS 39205
The Mississippi Department of Archives and History, through the Mississippi State Historical Museum, focuses attention on the folk arts by providing exhibits, film and video documentaries, and publications to organizations on request. The Mississippi

Arts Commission provides a Folk Arts Apprenticeship Program and an Individual Folk Artist Fellowship in the form of grants.

Missouri Arts Council
Wainwright State Office Complex
111 North 7th Street, Suite 105
St. Louis, MO 63101
The Missouri Arts Council, in partnership with the Missouri Cultural Heritage Center at the University of Missouri-Columbia, sponsors the Traditional Arts Apprenticeship Program. This program provides opportunities for qualified students to learn style, technique, and repertoire from recognized traditional master artists in all arts areas.

Missouri Cultural Heritage Center
University of Missouri
Conley House
Conley & Sanford Streets
Columbia, MO 65211
The Missouri Cultural Heritage Center serves as a clearinghouse for information on cultural resource activities; develops research projects exploring local and regional heritage; sponsors public programs such as exhibits, workshops, and lectures; and produces a newsletter and publication series. It also assists in coordinating the Traditional Arts Apprenticeship Program with the Missouri Arts Council.

North Carolina Arts Council
Department of Cultural Resources
Raleigh, NC 27611
The Folklife Section of the North Carolina Arts Council is a major resource center and programming agency. It seeks out craftspeople and brings their work to the public through documentation and exhibition. Programs range from statewide festivals to workshops and classroom presentations, with some grant money available.

South Carolina Arts Commission
1800 Gervais Street, Columbia, SC 29201
The South Carolina Arts Commission provides funding for organizations, people, and artists to promote both traditional and contemporary arts.

South Carolina Folk Arts Program
McKissick Museum
University of South Carolina
Columbia, SC 29208
The Folk Arts Program seeks to promote

the preservation of traditional arts in South Carolina by offering technical assistance, research, and public presentations. While not a granting agency, it does have extensive research facilities in its resource center.

State Arts Council of Oklahoma
Jim Thorpe Building, Room 640
Oklahoma City, OK 73105
The State Arts Council of Oklahoma encourages and stimulates all forms of artistic endeavor, assists organizations in making the arts accessible to the people of the state, and expands interest in the arts. Through its Artists in Residence Program, folk artists can give hands-on demonstrations of techniques.

Tennessee Arts Commission
Folk Arts Program
320 6th Avenue North, Suite 100
Nashville, TN 37219
The Folk Arts Program of the Tennessee Arts Commission provides information and technical assistance concerning folklife in Tennessee. It has a limited grant program and initiates special projects. It also houses files on folk art resources, organizations, and activities in Tennessee.

Texas Folklife Resources
P.O. Box 49824, Austin, TX 78765
Texas Folklife Resources is a nonprofit statewide service organization for the preservation and presentation of Texas folklife and folk art. It identifies and documents living Texas folk artists, encourages professional and comprehensive approaches to the preservation and presentation of folk art, promotes the study of folklore and folklife, and advocates the development of public policy that recognizes the importance of maintaining the rich cultural heritage of Texas.

West Virginia Department of Culture and History
Cultural Center, Capitol Complex
Charleston, WV 25305
The Department of Culture and History serves as a channel for funding and advice for folk festivals and also serves as a clearinghouse for grant information.

And also:

National Endowment for the Arts
Folk Arts Program
1100 Pennsylvania Avenue, NW

Washington, DC 20506
The Folk Arts Program of the National Endowment for the Arts supports traditional arts activities, particularly those that take place within the communities where those folk arts are practiced. It provides grants to nonprofit organizations for statewide apprenticeship programs and to present traditional folk arts in festivals, concerts, exhibits, and workshops both in person and through film or videotape. It also funds state and local government agencies with similar purposes.

Magazines & Journals

In addition to those published by regional folklore clubs and societies, the following magazines and journals publish articles that cover a variety of traditional crafts, some more regularly than others. Write to them for subscription information.

Alabama Folklife Association Newsletter
Alabama Folklife Association
University of Alabama
P.O. Box 1391, University, AL 35486

American Craft
American Craft Council
401 Park Avenue South
New York, NY 10016

American Indian Basketry
P.O. Box 66124, Portland, OR 97266

Appalachian Journal
Appalachian State University
Boone, NC 28608

Appalachian South
Appalachian Associates
P.O. Box 5, Pipestem, WV 25979

Archives of Appalachia Newsletter
East Tennessee State University
Sherrod Library
P.O. Box 22450-A
Johnson City, TN 37614

Arkansas Folklore Society Newsletter
Arkansas Folklore Society
University of Arkansas
P.O. Box 2748, Fayetteville, AR 72701

Artifacts
South Carolina Arts Commission
1800 Gervais Street, Columbia, SC 29201

Back Home in Kentucky
Cockrel Corporation
Route 9, Box 10
Bowling Green, KY 42101

Clarion
Museum of American Folk Art
55 West 53rd Street, New York, NY 10019

Cotton Patch Rag
Houston Folklore Society
6614 Del Rio, Houston, TX 77201

Delaware History
Historical Society of Delaware
505 Market Street
Wilmington, DE 19801

Florida Folklife News
Florida Folklife Program
P.O. Box 265, White Springs, FL 32096

Folklife
Arkansas Arts Council
225 East Markham Street
Little Rock, AR 72201

Folklife Center News
American Folklife Center
Library of Congress
Washington, DC 20560

Goldenseal Magazine
Department of Culture and History
Cultural Center, Capitol Complex
Charleston, WV 25305

Indiana Folklore
Hoosier Folklore Society
504 North Fess Street
Bloomington, IN 47401

Journal of American Culture
Bowling Green State University
Popular Culture Center
Bowling Green, OH 43403

Journal of Cherokee Studies
Museum of the Cherokee Indian
P.O. Box 770-A, Cherokee, NC 28719

Kentucky Folklore Record
Kentucky Folklore Society
Western Kentucky University
Box U-169, Bowling Green, KY 42101

Louisiana Folklore Newsletter
Louisiana Folklore Society
Department of English
Louisiana State University
Baton Rouge, LA 70803

Ozark Crafts
Ozark Regional Crafts Association
P.O. Box 800, Mountain View, AR 72560

Southern Folklore Quarterly
University of Florida
Gainesville, FL 32611

Southern Register
University of Mississippi
Center for the Study of Southern Culture
University, MS 38677

Studies in Traditional American Crafts
435 Main Street
P.O. Box 415, Oneida, NY 13421

West Virginia Folklore Journal
West Virginia Folklore Society
P.O. Box 446, Fairmont, WV 26554

Museums

The following listing includes institutions throughout the South that exhibit traditional crafts in standard museum settings, as well as living farm and village museums that feature regional handmade artifacts and demonstrations of traditional craft techniques. Many are open seasonally or on certain days of the week, so be sure to check before visiting. A dagger (†) indicates that the building is accessible to the handicapped; two daggers (††) indicate that the building is partially accessible to the handicapped.

Acadian Village
Route 3, Box 1976, Lafayette, LA 70506
(318) 981-2489
The museum offers an authentic view of nineteenth century Acadian life through restored homes with period furnishings and craft items.

Americana Museum
401 Aurora Avenue
Terra Alta, WV 26764
(304) 789-2361
The five-building living museum features artifacts and puts on demonstrations, such as how to spin yarn on a spinning wheel. †

Berea College Appalachian Museum
Berea College
C.P.O. 2298, Berea, KY 40404
(606) 986-9341 ext. 6078
The changing collection of more than 2,500 objects includes tools, toys, and utensils of everyday life in the past. The museum, which dates from 1926, has prepared displays and audiovisual programs showing craftsmen making traditional craft items and occasionally live demonstrations. †

Blue Ridge Farm Museum
Blue Ridge Institute
Ferrum College, Ferrum, VA 24088

(703) 365-2121 ext. 416
A re-created farmstead illustrates the early settlements of the Blue Ridge and the development of a distinct regional agricultural way of life. The Blue Ridge Farm Museum presents the history and culture of early Virginia settlements in the southwestern mountains of the state. †

Cherokee National Museum
P.O. Box 515, Tahlequah, OK 74465
(918) 456-6007
The Cherokee National Museum presents the Cherokee story from man's arrival on the North American continent to the present day. Exhibits include Indian artifacts from prehistoric as well as more recent times. †

Exchange Place Restoration
4812 Orebank Road
Kingsport, TN 37664
(615) 288-3452
This living farm complex of the 1850s features a variety of crafts with an emphasis on craft demonstrations. †

Fort New Salem
Salem College, Salem, WV 26426
(304) 782-5245
Through craftmaking, music, storytelling, regional foods, artifacts, and much more, this museum interprets the early frontier settlement period of the Appalachian region from 1790–1830. †

Georgia Agrirama
P.O. Box Q, Tifton, GA 31793
(912) 386-3344
The rural heritage of the daily activities of the late 1800s is displayed in three distinct areas: rural town, industrial sites complex, and farmsteading communities. More than 25 structures have been relocated to the 70-acre site and faithfully restored or preserved as they appeared in that era. ††

Havre de Grace Decoy Museum
P.O. Box A, Foot of Giles Street
Havre de Grace, MD 21078
(301) 939-3739 or 939-3833
The collection includes handcrafted decoys from the Upper Chesapeake Bay region, a life-like display created from a 1942 workshop showing local carvers Madison Mitchell, Paul Gibson, Bob McGaw, and Lou Klair; and a wet display and workshop. †

Homespun Museum
Grovewood Road, Asheville, NC 28804
(704) 253-7651
Housed in the Biltmore Industries gatehouse, this museum features the homespun industries and a variety of traditional crafts made in North Carolina within the last century.†

Lauren Rogers Museum of Art
P.O. Box 1108, Laurel, MS 39441
(601) 649-6374
This museum houses a large collection of American Indian baskets.†

McKissick Museum
University of South Carolina
Columbia, SC 29208
(803) 777-7251
Housed here are examples of alkaline- and salt-glazed pottery from North and South Carolina, an extensive collection of seagrass baskets originating from the South Carolina low country, Catawba Indian pottery, and other Southern folk art. The museum's textile holdings contain nineteenth- and early twentieth-century clothing (dresses, suits, aprons, bonnets), table scarves, and cloths and quilts from throughout the Carolinas.†

Miccosukee Indian Village
P.O. Box 440021, Tamiami Station
Miami, FL 33144
(305) 223-8380
In the crafts area of this museum, men and women demonstrate different techniques, including the carving of cypress or willow branches into children's toys.†

Mingei International Museum of World Folk Art
P.O. Box 553, La Jolla, CA 92038
(619) 453-5300
The Mingei locates, collects, and documents historical and contemporary world folk art and crafts, which are used in specialized exhibitions and publications. Three to four major exhibitions are presented each year and are accompanied by authentic folk music, illustrated lectures, films, and other educational events.†

Mint Museum
2730 Randolph, Charlotte, NC 28207
(704) 337-2000
While the Mint Museum is generally an art museum, it does collect some historic folk crafts and contemporary crafts by artists in the Southeastern region. It also has a 2,000-piece collection of pottery produced in North Carolina in the past 150 years.†

Mississippi State Historical Museum
Old Capitol Restoration
100 South State Street
Jackson, MS 39201
(601) 354-6222
Highlights of the museum's folk art holdings include a diverse collection of traditional crafts from the Mississippi region.†

Mountain Heritage Center
Western Carolina University
Cullowhee, NC 28723
(704) 227-7129
This museum has artifacts representing Southern Appalachian life from prehistoric times to the twentieth century.†

Museum of American Folk Art
444 Park Avenue South
New York, NY 10016
(212) 481-3080
The Museum of American Folk Art is closed until 1989, pending construction of a new building. Call or write for information on temporary and traveling exhibitions.

Museum of Appalachia
P.O. Box 359, Norris, TN 37828
(615) 494-7680
Housing nearly 250,000 items, this museum of early American and pioneer items in authentic settings offers a glimpse of life in the past.†

Museum of Early Southern Decorative Arts
P.O. Box 10310
Winston-Salem, NC 27108
(919) 722-6148
This museum, dedicated to exhibiting and researching the regional decorative arts of the early South, is composed of nineteen period rooms and six galleries. The collections include materials made and used in Maryland, Virginia, the Carolinas, Georgia, Kentucky, and Tennessee through 1820.†

Museum of the Cherokee Indian
P.O. Box 770-A, Cherokee, NC 28719
(704) 497-3481
This museum features an extensive collection of Cherokee Indian artifacts with an emphasis on the era before the tribe's "removal" to Oklahoma.†

North American Wildfowl Art Museum
655 South Salisbury Boulevard
Salisbury, MD 21801
(800) 742-4988
This museum has one of America's finest public collections of antique decorative bird carvings and decoys representing the major waterfowling areas of the East Coast and the Midwest. The collection is arranged chronologically, so the visitor can follow the development of the art from the crude reed decoys used by the American Indians, to the simple, graceful working decoys of the market gunners of the 1800s, to the intricate, complex sculptures being made by leading artists today.†

Oscar Farris Tennessee Agricultural Museum
Ellington Agricultural Center
P.O. Box 40627, Nashville, TN 37204
The Oscar Farris Agricultural Museum displays an extensive collection of artifacts used daily by Tennessee's farm families in the 1800s and early 1900s.†

San Francisco Craft and Folk Art Museum
Landmark Building A
Fort Mason, San Francisco, CA 94123
(415) 775-0990
This museum's exhibits are changed six times a year, highlighting folk art and traditional crafts from around the world.†

Seagrove Pottery Museum
P.O. Box 123, Seagrove, NC 27341
No telephone.
This museum exhibits wares from the early years of the area's pottery production to the present.†

Shaker Village of Pleasant Hill
Route 3, Harrodsburg, KY 40330
(606) 734-5411
The Shaker Village of Pleasant Hill preserves 30 original nineteenth-century buildings accurately restored and adapted to provide visitors a variety of rewarding experiences. There are demonstrations by spinners, weavers, and broommakers, and music and craft programs.

Southern Plains Indian Museum
P.O. Box 749, Anadarko, OK 73005
(405) 247-6221
This museum is a permanent exhibit presenting the rich diversity of historic arts of the tribal peoples of western Oklahoma.†

University Museums
University of Mississippi
University, MS 38677
(601) 232-7073
Located on the University of Mississippi campus at Oxford, the museum includes an extensive collection of Afro-American quilts and other objects.†

Zebulon B. Vance Birthplace
State Historic Site
911 Reems Creek Road
Weaverville, NC 28787
(704) 645-6706
This site is a pioneer farmstead made up of a five-room reconstructed log house and six outbuildings furnished to represent the period from 1790 to 1840.††

Westville Historic Handicrafts, Inc.
P.O. Box 1850, Lumpkin, GA 31815
(912) 838-6310
Westville is a functioning living history village of authentically restored, original buildings and landscaping. The Village of Westville realistically depicts Georgia's preindustrial life and culture of 1850.††

Winterthur Museum and Gardens
Winterthur, DE 19735
(302) 656-8591
This museum houses a collection of American decorative and fine arts, including Shaker items, from the period 1640–1840.†

Films & Videotapes
The following films and videotapes on various aspects of traditional crafts are available for rental and/or purchase. Write to the distributing companies listed below for current pricing and availability.

Alex Stewart: Cooper
Available in 16mm, 13 minutes
Available for rental or purchase from:
Instructional Media Center
East Tennessee State University
Box 22570A, Johnson City, TN 37614

Appalachian Toymakers
Available in ¾" cassette; ½" reel-to-reel; ½" cassette (Beta I or II; VHS I or II), 25 minutes
Available for rental or purchase from:
Primalux Video
30 West 26th Street
New York, NY 10010

Apple Dolls
Available in 16mm and videotape;
¾" cassette and ½" cassette, 19 minutes

Available for rental from:
Wombat Productions
250 West 57th Street, Suite 916
New York, NY 10019

Basket Builder
Available in 16mm, 12 minutes
Available for rental from:
Blue Ridge Films
9003 Glenbrook Road
Fairfax, VA 22030

Black Indians of New Orleans
Available in 16mm and in video,
33 minutes
Available for rental or purchase from:
Cote Blanche Productions
Route 3, Box 614, Cut Off, LA 70345

The Cooper's Craft
Available in 16mm; ½″ VHS or Beta I, II;
or ¾″ U-Matic, 39 minutes (16mm);
28½ minutes (video)
Available for rental (16mm) or purchase
(16mm or video) from:
Colonial Williamsburg
AV Distribution Section
Box C, Williamsburg, VA 23187

Corn Husk Dolls
Available in 16mm, 10 minutes
Available for rental or purchase from:
Bill Snyder Films
P.O. Box 2784, Fargo, ND 58102

Creative Hands
Available in 16mm, 12 minutes
Available for rental or purchase from:
Filmfair Communications
10900 Ventura Boulevard
P.O. Box 1728, Studio City, CA 91604

Edd Presnell: Dulcimer Maker
Available in 16mm, 6 minutes
Available for rental or purchase from:
Instructional Media Center
East Tennessee State University
Box 22570A, Johnson City, TN 37614

The Fiddler
Available in 16mm, 25 minutes
Available for rental or purchase from:
Family Films
14622 Lanark Street
Panorama City, CA 91402

Four Women Artists
Available in 16mm and ¾″ cassette,
25 minutes
Available for rental or purchase from:
Center for Southern Folklore

1216 Peabody Avenue
P.O. Box 4081, Memphis, TN 38104

Gravel Springs Fife and Drum
Available in 16mm, 10 minutes
Available for rental or purchase from:
Center for Southern Folklore
1216 Peabody Avenue
P.O. Box 4081, Memphis, TN 38104

Hand Carved
Available in 16mm and VHS cassette,
88 minutes
Available for rental or purchase from:
Appalshop Films
P.O. Box 743, Whitesburg, KY 41858

Leon "Peck" Clark—Basketmaker
Available in 16mm and ¾″ cassette,
15 minutes
Available for rental or purchase from:
Center for Southern Folklore
1216 Peabody Avenue, P.O. Box 4081
Memphis, TN 38104

*Martha Mitchell of Possum Walk Road:
Quiltmaker*
Available in ½″ VHS or Beta and
¾″ U-Matic, 30 minutes
Available for purchase only from:
Melvin R. Mason
Department of English
Sam Houston State University
Huntsville, TX 77341

*Missing Pieces: Contemporary Georgia
Folk Art*
Available in 16mm, 28 minutes
Available for rental or purchase from:
Georgia Council for the Arts
and Humanities
2082 East Exchange Place, Suite 100
Tucker, GA 30084

*1985 National Rolley Hole Marbles
Championships*
Available in video, 50 minutes
Available for rental or purchase from:
Dragon Productions
Livingston, TN 38570

Oaksie
Available in 16mm, 22 minutes
Available for rental or purchase from:
Appalshop Films
P.O. Box 743, Whitesburg, KY 41858

Ott Blair: Sled Maker
Available in 16mm, 5 minutes
Available for rental or purchase from:
Instructional Media Center

East Tennessee State University
Box 22570A, Johnson City, TN 37614

Quilting Party
Available in 16mm and video, 3 minutes
Available for rental or purchase from:
Trio Films
Route 2, Box 213-A
Mebane, NC 27302

Quilting Women
Available in 16mm, 28 minutes
Available for rental or purchase from:
Appalshop Films
P.O. Box 743, Whitesburg, KY 41858

Quilts in Women's Lives
Available in 16mm or ½″ cassette,
28 minutes
Available for rental (16mm only) or purchase (16mm or video) from:
New Day Films
22 Riverview Drive, Wayne, NJ 07470

*Sheep, Shearing and Spinning: A Story of
Wool*
Available in 16mm or VHS cassette,
11 minutes
Available for rental or purchase from:
International Film Bureau
332 South Michigan Avenue
Chicago, IL 60604-4382

Sourwood Mountain Dulcimers
Available in 16mm, 28 minutes
Available for rental or purchase from:
Appalshop Films
P.O. Box 743, Whitesburg, KY 41858

Under the Covers
Available in 16mm; ½″ VHS or Beta II;
and ¾″ U-Matic, 11 minutes
Available for rental or purchase from:
Pyramid Film and Video
P.O. Box 1048
Santa Monica, CA 90406

Festivals

Of the annual festivals listed below, some
are events that offer strictly traditional
activities, and others are celebrations
that include traditional elements in their
festivities. Because the exact dates vary
from year to year, it is advisable to con-
tact the sponsoring organization for specific date and time information.

Winter Festivals

Americana Sampler
Nashville, TN

First or second weekend in February
For information:
P.O. Box 8222, Nashville, TN 37207

Annual Tribal Festival and Rodeo
Hollywood, FL
Second weekend in February
For information:
Seminole Tribe of Florida
6073 Stirling Road
Hollywood, FL 33024

Indian Arts Festival
Miami, FL
Last week in December
For information:
Miccosukee Tribe of Florida
P.O. Box 440021, Tamiami Station
Miami, FL 33144

Spring Festivals

Annual Arkansas Folk Festival
Mountain View, AR
Third weekend in April
For information:
Ozark Folk Center
P.O. Box 500
Mountain View, AR 72560

Annual Georgia Folk Festival
Eatonton, GA
Memorial Day weekend
For information:
Rock Eagle 4-H Club Center
350 Rock Eagle Road NW
Eatonton, GA 31024

Annual Historic Rural Life Festival
Nashville, TN
Second week in May
For information:
Oscar Farris Tennessee Agricultural
Museum
Ellington Agricultural Center
P.O. Box 40627, Nashville, TN 37204

Annual World Gee Haw Whimmy
Diddle Championship
Asheville, NC
Late spring or early summer
For information:
Southern Highland Handicraft Guild
P.O. Box 9545, Asheville, NC 28815

Cotton Pickin' Country Fair
Gay, GA
First weekends in May and October
For information:
Cotton Pickin' Fairs
P.O. Box 1, Gay, GA 30218

Florida Folk Festival
White Springs, FL
Memorial Day weekend
For information:
Bureau of Florida Folklife
P.O. Box 265, White Springs, FL 32096

Folk Arts Festival
Kingsport, TN
Last weekend in April; third weekend in
September
For information:
Exchange Place Restoration
4812 Orebank Road
Kingsport, TN 37664

Gullah Festival of South Carolina
Beaufort, SC
Memorial Day weekend
For information:
P.O. Box 83, Beaufort, SC 29901

Havre de Grace Decoy Festival
Havre de Grace, MD
First weekend in May
For information:
Havre de Grace Decoy Museum
P.O. Box A, Havre de Grace, MD 21078

Mossy Creek Barnyard Arts and Crafts
Festival
Warner Robins, GA
Third weekends in April and October
For information:
Barnyard Arts and Crafts
106 Anne Drive
Warner Robins, GA 31093

New Orleans Jazz and Heritage Festival
New Orleans, LA
Last weekend in April; first weekend
in May
For information, send SASE to:
1205 North Rampart Street
New Orleans, LA 70116

Northern Virginia Folk Festival
Arlington, VA
Second weekend in May
For information:
2700 South Lang Street
Arlington, VA 22206

Olde Country Folk Festival
Silver Dollar City
Branson, MO
Last two weeks in May
For information:
Silver Dollar City
Marvel Cave Park, MO 65616

Prater's Mill Country Fair
Dalton, GA
Second weekends in May and October
For information:
Prater's Mill Foundation
101 Timberland Drive
Dalton, GA 30721

Vandalia Gathering
Charleston, WV
Third weekend in May
For information:
West Virginia Department of Culture
and History
Cultural Center, Capitol Complex
Charleston, WV 25305

War Eagle Fair
War Eagle, AR
First Friday in May; third Friday in
October
For information:
Ozark Arts and Crafts Fair Association
Route 1, Box 157, Hindsville, AR 72738

Summer Festivals

Americana Summer Sampler
Nashville, TN
First weekend in August
For information:
Americana Sampler, Inc.
P.O. Box 8222, Nashville, TN 37207

Annual Guild Fair
Asheville, NC
Third weekend in July; third weekend in
October
For information:
Southern Highland Handicraft Guild
P.O. Box 9545, Asheville, NC 28815

Appalachian Celebration
Morehead, KY
Last full week in June
For information:
Coordinator of Special Projects
Office of Regional Development Services
Morehead State University
Morehead, KY 40351

Augusta Festival
Elkins, WV
Second weekend in August
For information:
Augusta Heritage Center
Davis and Elkins College
Elkins, WV 26241

Black Belt Folk Roots Festival
Eutaw, AL

Fourth weekend in August
For information:
P.O. Box 809, Eutaw, AL 35462

Choctaw Indian Fair
Philadelphia, MS
First Wednesday, Thursday, Friday, and
Saturday after July 4
For information:
Route 7, Box 21
Philadelphia, MS 39350

Festival of American Folklife
Washington, DC
Last week in June and first week in July
For information:
Office of Folklife Programs
Smithsonian Institution
955 L'Enfant Plaza, Suite 2600
Washington, DC 20560

Folklife Festival—Warrior's Path
State Park
Kingsport, TN
Last Saturday in July
For information:
Warrior's Path State Park
P.O. Box 5026, Kingsport, TN 37663

Haywood County Smoky Mountain
Folk Festival
Waynesville, NC
First weekend in July
For information:
Waynesville Parks and Recreation
Department
217 West Marshall Street
Waynesville, NC 28786

Kentucky Music Weekend
Louisville, KY
First weekend in August
For information:
P.O. Box 651, Bardstown, KY 40004

Mountain State Art and Craft Fair
Ripley, WV
Five days including July 4
For information:
P.O. Box 389, Ripley, WV 25271

Natchitoches-Northwestern
Folk Festival
Natchitoches, LA
Third weekend in July
For information:
P.O. Box 3663, Northwestern State
University
Natchitoches, LA 71497

National Rolley Hole Marbles
Championship

Livingston, TN
First weekend in August
For information:
Route 1, Box 500, Lake City, TN 37769

Pioneer Days and Wheat Harvest
Point Pleasant, WV
Third weekend in June
For information:
West Virginia State Farm Museum
Route 1, Box 479
Point Pleasant, WV 25550

Texas Folklife Festival
San Antonio, TX
First weekend in August
For information:
University of Texas Institute
of Texan Cultures
P.O. Box 1226, San Antonio, TX 78294

West Virginia State Folk Festival
Glenville, WV
Third weekend in June
For information:
Route 78, Box 25, Linn, WV 26384

Fall Festivals

Annual Harvest Festival
Mountain View, AR
Second through last weekends in
October
For information:
Ozark Folk Center
P.O. Box 500
Mountain View, AR 72560

Annual Fall Mountain Heritage Arts and
Crafts Festival
Charles Town, WV
Last weekend in September
For information:
P.O. Box 426, Charles Town, WV 25414

Annual John Henry Folk Festival
Pipestem, WV
Labor Day weekend
For information:
P.O. Box 135, Princeton, WV 24740

Annual Labor Day Pirogue Race Festival
Houma, LA
Labor Day weekend
For information:
P.O. Box 2792, Houma, LA 70361

Backwood Folk Festival
Highway 126, between Dodson and
Readhimer, LA
Second Friday and Saturday in
September

RESOURCES

INDEX

PHOTO CREDITS

All photographs were taken by the author, with the following exceptions:

All studio photography on white background by John Beckman.

p. 16, by Doris Ulmann. Ulmann Collection, University of Oregon Library.

p. 18, photographer unknown. Valentine Museum, Richmond, Virginia.

p. 29, by Robert Cogswell, from the Folk Arts in Rural Libraries Project. Courtesy of the Kentucky Department of Libraries and Archives and the Kentucky Arts Council, Frankfort, Kentucky.

p. 37, by Leigh Richmond Miner. Penn School Historical Collection. Permission granted by Penn Community Services, Inc., St. Helena Island, South Carolina.

p. 38, by Dale Rosengarten, McClellenville, South Carolina.

p. 61, by Ray Allen. Courtesy of the Tennessee State Library and Archive, Nashville, Tennessee.

p. 64, National Museum of American Art, Smithsonian Institution, Washington, D.C.

p. 78, photographer unknown. Hindman Settlement School Photographic Collection, Berea College Southern Appalachian Archives.

p. 84, by Ray Allen. Courtesy of the Tennessee State Library and Archives, Nashville, Tennessee.

pp. 88, 89, by William Ferris. Courtesy of Special Collections, University of Mississippi.

p. 90, by Doris Ulmann. Ulmann Collection, University of Oregon Library.

p. 92 right top and bottom, courtesy Texas Folklife Resources, Austin, Texas.

p. 93, by Doris Ulmann. Ulmann Collection, University of Oregon Library.

p. 94 left, top right, middle bottom, by Ray Allen. Courtesy of the Tennessee State Library and Archive.

p. 94 bottom right, by Robert Cogswell, from the Folk Arts in Rural Libraries Project. Courtesy of the Kentucky Department of Libraries and Archives and the Kentucky Arts Council, Frankfort, Kentucky.

p. 97, by Greg Guirard, St. Martinville, Louisiana.

p. 102, by Ricky Saltzman. Courtesy of the Art Department, University of Mississippi.

p. 107, by William Ferris. Courtesy of Special Collections, University of Mississippi.

p. 109, by Doris Ulmann. Used with special permission from Berea College and the Doris Ulmann Foundation.

pp. 112, 113, by William Ferris. Courtesy of Special Collections, University of Mississippi.

p. 114, by Ricky Saltzman. Courtesy of Art Department, University of Mississippi.

p. 115, courtesy Texas Folklife Resources, Austin, Texas.

p. 137, by Doris Ulmann. Ulmann Collection, University of Oregon Library.

pp. 138, 139, by Robert Cogswell, from the Folk Arts in Rural Libraries Project. Courtesy of the Kentucky Department of Libraries and Archives and the Kentucky Arts Council, Frankfort, Kentucky.

p. 140, by Ray Allen. Courtesy of the Tennessee State Library and Archive, Nashville, Tennessee.

p. 141, by Ray Allen. Courtesy of the Center for Southern Folklore, Memphis, Tennessee.

p. 143, by William Ferris. Courtesy of Special Collections, University of Mississippi.

p. 144, left, by Robert Cogswell, from the Folk Arts in Rural Libraries Project. Courtesy of the Kentucky Department of Libraries and Archives and the Kentucky Arts Council, Nashville, Tennessee.

p. 144 right, photographer unknown. Courtesy of Tennessee State Library and Archive, Nashville, Tennessee.

p. 150 left, photographer unknown. John C. Campbell Folk School Photographic Collection, Berea College Southern Appalachian Archives.

p. 162 left, by Betty Belanus. Courtesy of the Tennessee State Library and Archive, Nashville, Tennessee.

pp. 162 right, 163, 164 left, by Robert Cogswell, from the Folk Arts in Rural Libraries Project. Courtesy of the Kentucky Department of Libraries and Archives and the Kentucky Arts Council, Frankfort, Kentucky.

p. 169 left, by Doris Ulmann. Used with special permission from Berea College and the Doris Ulmann Foundation.

p. 184 left, by Robert Cogswell, from the Folk Arts in Rural Libraries Project. Courtesy of the Kentucky Department of Libraries and Archives and the Kentucky Arts Council.

p. 184 right, 185, by Greg Guirard, St. Martinville, Louisiana.

p. 197, by Ray Allen. Courtesy of Art Department, the University of Mississippi.

p. 198, 200 top right, 201 bottom, courtesy of Texas Folklife Resources, Austin, Texas.

p. 216, photographer unknown. Courtesy Georgia Department of Archives and History, Atlanta, Georgia.

ACKNOWLEDGMENTS

As with most projects of this enormity, the research, writing, and photographing of *By Southern Hands* would not have been possible without the help and encouragement of many people. To the following scholars, experts, colleagues, collectors, and friends, I offer my profound respect and sincerest appreciation:

Gail Antle; Ifama Arsan, Blake and Nancy Barker; John Beckman; Audrey Bernard; Harry Bickle; Ferdinand Bigard; Martha Boynton; Ray Brassieur; Sam Bush; C.I.S. Professional Women's Group; Charles Camp; Martha Neal Cooke; Frances Drummond; Elaine Eff; Nora Fine; Mildred Franks; Sharon Freedman; Ralph and Sally Gates; Dennis Gibson; Glenn Gilmore; Margaret Gorove; Walter Hyleck; Robert Gray; Duane Henry; Janet Higgens; George Holt; David Horvath and my friends at the University of Louisville Photographic Archive; Loyal Jones; Craig Kaviar; Ed Klee; Vicky Ledford; Jack Leonard and my friends at Shaker Village of Pleasant Hill; the staff at Locust Grove Historic Home in Kentucky; Ronni Lundy; Georgie Manuel; Charles Martin; Richard McAllister; Betty Morris; Pat Morris; Al Muller; Jim O'Neal; Gerald Parsons; C.J. Pressma; Zachary Richard; Pat Ross; Jane Sapp; Sharron Sarthou; Julie Segal; Laura Sims; George Terry; Helen Thompson; Lucy Turnbull; Richard Van Kleeck; Debbie Von Bokern; Maude Southwell Wahlman; Bridgett and Ted Wathen; Henry Willett; Charles Wolfe; and Shelly Zegart.

In addition, to the following people I offer a special thank you:

To the Pentax Corporation for their generous support of Pentax 645 equipment for this project;

To Betsy Adler of the Kentucky Humanities Council; Robert Cogswell, now the Director of Folk Arts for the Tennessee Arts Commission; Burt Feintuch, coordinator of the Programs in Folk Studies at Western Kentucky University; and Ann Ogden of the Kentucky Arts Council, my warmest appreciation for spending valuable time with me many years ago at the inception of this project, helping me to determine my direction and focus;

To Bob Conway, formerly of the North Carolina Division of Archives and History, and his wife, Arlene, owner of the Appalachian Craft Center in Asheville; Betty DuPree, manager of the Qualla Arts and Crafts Mutual in Cherokee, North Carolina; William Ferris, Director of the Center for the Study of Southern Culture at the University of Mississippi; Greg Guirard, photographer extraordinaire in St. Martinville, Louisiana; Pat Jasper and Betsy Peterson of Texas Folklife Resources in Austin; Paul Newby in McMinnville, Tennessee; Roy Parfait, able spokesperson for the Houma Indians in Dulac, Louisiana; and Dale Rosengarten, historian and friend to Gullah basketsewers, in McClellenville, South Carolina, for their seemingly boundless enthusiasm and energy on behalf of their regions' traditional craftspeople, and their willing graciousness in sharing them with me;

To Virginia Croft, who edited the manuscript, and to Ron Gross, who designed the book, for transforming my words and pictures into a remarkable and stunning partnership;

To my close friends Gloria and Al Needlman who read each word as it was written, listened to the stories, and offered encouragement all along the way;

To Marsha Melnick and Susan E. Meyer of Roundtable Press in New York, and to Oxmoor House in Birmingham, Alabama, for believing in me and for allowing me the requisite freedom to pursue this personal odyssey;

To my research assistant, Jim Young, whose insatiable appetite for searching, fastidious accuracy in helping me keep track of the incredible amount of information, and unflagging dedication to this project were a daily motivator in completing *By Southern Hands*;

To my small children, Samuel, Abraham, and Chloe Hawkins, in whose hands, along with those of all American children, is left the legacy of traditional crafts, for their wonder and innate understanding of the worth of handmade goods, their patience with our erratic travel and work schedule, and their unconditional love at all times;

To my husband, Mark Hawkins, who steadfastly maintained his confidence in me, and without whose help and love this book would never have been completed;

And, finally, to all the craftspeople throughout the South who unselfishly opened their homes and hearts to me. It is my deepest wish that the curiosity and interest shown in their work will serve to perpetuate their traditions for generations to come.